THE PATH OF INSIGHT MEDITATION

JOSEPH GOLDSTEIN
AND JACK KORNFIELD

THE PATH OF INSIGHT MEDITATION

SHAMBHALA
Boston & London
1995

Shambhala Publications, Inc.
Horticultural Hall
300 Massachusetts Avenue
Boston, Massachusetts 02115

9 8 7 6 5 4 3 2 1

Printed in Hong Kong on acid-free paper
Distributed in the United States by Random House, Inc.,
and in Canada by Random House of Canada Ltd

See page 178 for Library of Congress
Cataloging-in-Publication data.

CONTENTS

PREFACE

The Path of Insight Meditation was born out of the authors' twelve-year collaboration in teaching vipassana meditation retreats throughout the world. These intensive retreats, ranging in length from weekends to three months, provide opportunities for a simple and direct investigation of the mind and body. Through the development of concentrated awareness, insight into the changing nature of phenomena deepens in a very personal and immediate way. This, in turn, leads to an understanding of the causes of suffering in ourselves and others and to the possibility of compassion and genuine freedom.

The book offers a clear explanation of the meditation instructions and exercises that are given on retreats. While its flavor and emphasis are drawn from silent retreat practice, the teachings are also set in a broad context that makes meditation practice meaningful and relevant in our lives. These teachings are strongly rooted in the Buddhist tradition, especially as it has developed and flowered in Thailand and Burma. Two of the main lineages that have been interwoven throughout the book are the forest monastic tradition of Ven. Achaan Chaa and the practice of intensive satipathana vipassana meditation as taught by the late Ven. Mahasi Sayadaw. Together they help to provide the breadth of perspective and depth of understanding that characterize the wisdom of the Buddha.

Readers who desire information about Buddhist insight meditation retreats and teaching worldwide may contact the Insight Meditation Society, Pleasant Street, Barre, Massachusetts 01005 or Spirit Rock Meditation Center, P.O. Box 904, Woodacre, California 94973.

EDITOR'S NOTE

This book consists of selected chapters from *Seeking the Heart of Wisdom,* by Joseph Goldstein and Jack Kornfield (Boston & London: Shambhala Publications, 1987).

THE PATH OF INSIGHT MEDITATION

1

DISCOVERING THE HEART OF MEDITATION

It is said that soon after his enlightenment, the Buddha passed a man on the road who was struck by the extraordinary radiance and peacefulness of his presence. The man stopped and asked, "My friend, what are you? Are you a celestial being or a god?"

"No," said the Buddha.

"Well, then, are you some kind of magician or wizard?"

Again the Buddha answered, "No."

"Are you a man?"

"No."

"Well, my friend, what then are you?"

The Buddha replied, "I am awake."

The name Buddha means "one who is awake," and it is this experience that is the very heart and essence of vipassana, or insight meditation. It offers a way of practice that can open us to see clearly our bodies, our hearts, our minds, and the world around us and develop a wise and compassionate way to relate to and understand them all. This practice of insight meditation comes from the original core of the Buddha's teachings as transmitted for 2,500 years in the Theravada tradition of southern Asia. But it is not an "Asian" practice. It is a practice by which anyone can awaken to the truth of life and become free.

Right Understanding

The path of awakening begins with a step the Buddha called right understanding.

Right understanding has two parts. To start with, it asks a question of our hearts. What do we really value, what do we really care about in this life? Our lives are quite short. Our childhood goes by very quickly, then adolescence and adult life go by. We can be complacent and let our lives disappear in a dream, or we can become aware. In the beginning of practice we must ask what is most important to us. When we're ready to die, what will we want to have done? What will we care about most? At the time of death, people who have tried to live consciously ask only one or two questions about their life: Did I learn to live wisely? Did I love well? We can begin by asking them now.

This is the beginning of right understanding: looking at our lives, seeing that they are impermanent and fleeting, and taking into account what matters to us most deeply. In the same way, we can look at the world around us, where there is a tremendous amount of suffering, war, poverty, and disease. Hundreds of millions of people are having a terrible, terrible time in Africa and Central America and India and Southeast Asia and even right here in North America. What does the world need to foster a safe and compassionate existence for all? Human suffering and hardship cannot be alleviated just by a simple change of government or a new monetary policy, although these things may help. On the deepest level, problems such as war and starvation are not solved by economics and politics alone. Their source is prejudice and fear in the human heart—and their solution also lies in the human heart. What the world needs most is people who are less bound by prejudice. It needs more love, more generosity, more mercy, more openness. The root of human problems is not a lack of resources but comes from the misunderstanding, fear, and separateness that can be found in the hearts of people.

Right understanding starts by acknowledging the suffering and difficulties in the world around us as well as in our own lives. Then it asks us to touch what we really value inside, to find what we really care about, and to use that as the basis of our spiritual practice. When we see that things are not quite right in the world and in ourselves, we also become aware of another possibility, of the potential for us to open to greater loving kindness and a deep intuitive wisdom. From our heart comes inspiration for the spiritual journey. For some of us this will come as a sense of the great possibility of living in an awake and free way. Others of us are brought to practice as a way to come to terms with the power of suffering in our life. Some are inspired to seek understanding through a practice of discovery and inquiry, while some intuitively sense a connection with the divine or are inspired to practice as a way to open the heart more fully. Whatever brings us to spiritual practice can become a flame in our heart that guides and protects us and brings us to true understanding.

Right understanding also requires from us a recognition and understanding of the law of karma. Karma is not just a mystical idea about something esoteric like past lives in Tibet. The term *karma* refers to the law of cause and effect. It means that what we do and how we act create our future experiences. If we are angry at many people, we start to live in a climate of hate. People will get angry at us in return. If we cultivate love, it returns to us. It's simply how the law works in our lives.

Someone asked a vipassana teacher, Ruth Dennison, if she could explain karma very simply. She said, "Sure. Karma means you don't get away with *nothing!*" Whatever we do, however we act, creates how we become, how we will be, and how the world will be around us. To understand karma is wonderful because within this law there are possibilities to change the direction of our lives. We can actually train ourselves and transform the climate in which we live. We can practice being more loving, more aware, more conscious, or whatever we want. We can practice in retreats or while driving or in the supermarket checkout line. If we practice kindness, then spontaneously we start to experience more and more kindness within us and from the world around us.

There's a story of the Sufi figure Mullah Nasruddin, who is both a fool and a wise man. He was out one day in his garden sprinkling bread crumbs around the flowerbeds. A neighbor came by and asked, "Mullah, why are you doing that?"

Nasruddin answered, "Oh, I do it to keep the tigers away."

The neighbor said, "But there aren't any tigers within thousands of miles of here."

Nasruddin replied, "Effective, isn't it?"

Spiritual practice is not a mindless repetition of ritual or prayer. It works through consciously realizing the law of cause and effect and aligning our lives to it. Perhaps we can sense the potential of awakening in ourselves, but we must also see that it doesn't happen by itself. There are laws that we can follow to actualize this potential. How we act, how we relate to ourselves, to our bodies, to the people around us, to our work, creates the kind of world we live in, creates our very freedom or suffering.

Over the years and throughout various cultures, many techniques and systems of

Buddhist practice have been developed to bring this aspiration to fruition, but the essence of awakening is always the same: to see clearly and directly the truth of our experience in each moment, to be aware, to be mindful. This practice is a systematic development and opening of awareness called by the Buddha the four foundations of mindfulness: awareness of the body, awareness of feelings, awareness of mental phenomena, and awareness of truths, of the laws of experience.

To succeed in the cultivation of mindfulness, said the Buddha, is the highest benefit, informing all aspects of our life. "Sandalwood and tagara are delicately scented and give a little fragrance, but the fragrance of virtue and a mind well trained rises even to the gods."

How are we to begin? *The Path of Purification,* an ancient Buddhist text and guide, was written in answer to a short poem:

> The world is entangled in a knot.
> Who can untangle the tangle?

It is to untangle the tangle that we begin meditation practice. To disentangle ourselves, to be free, requires that we train our attention. We must begin to see how we get caught by fear, by attachment, by aversion—caught by suffering. This means directing attention to our everyday experience and learning to listen to our bodies, hearts, and minds. We attain wisdom not by creating ideals but by learning to see things clearly, as they are.

What is meditation? It's a good question. There is no shortage of descriptions, theories, manuals, texts, and ideas about it. There are hundreds of schools of meditation, which include prayer, reflection, devotion, visualization, and myriad ways to calm and focus the mind. Insight meditation (and other disciplines like it) is particularly directed to bringing understanding to the mind and heart. It begins with a training of awareness and a process of inquiry in ourselves. From this point of view, asking, "What is meditation?" is really the same as asking, "What is the mind?" or "Who am I?" or "What does it mean to be alive, to be free?"—questions about the fundamental nature of life and death. We must answer these questions in our own experience, through a discovery in ourselves. This is the heart of meditation.

It is a wonderful thing to discover these answers. Otherwise, much of life is spent on automatic pilot. Many people pass through years of life driven by greed, fear, aggression, or endless grasping after security, affection, power, sex, wealth, pleasure, and fame. This endless cycle of seeking is what Buddhism calls samsara. It is rare that we take time to understand this life that we are given to work with. We're born, we grow older, and eventually we die; we enjoy, we suffer, we wake, we sleep—how quickly it all slips away. Awareness of the suffering involved in this process of life, of being born, growing old, and dying led the Buddha to question deeply how it comes about and how we can find freedom. That was the Buddha's question. That is where he began his practice. Each of us has our own way of posing this question. To understand ourselves and our life is the point of insight meditation: to understand and to be free.

There are several types of understanding. One type comes from reading the words of others. We have all read and stored away an enormous amount of information, even about spiritual matters. Although this kind of understanding is useful, it is still someone else's experience. Similarly there is the understanding that comes from being told by someone wise or experienced: "It's this way, friend." That too can be useful.

There is a deeper understanding based on our own consideration and reflection: "I've seen this through thoughtful analysis. I understand how it works." A tremendous amount can be known through thought. But is there a level deeper than that? What happens when we begin to ask the most fundamental questions about our lives? What is love? What is freedom? These questions cannot be answered by second-hand or intellectual ways of understanding. What the Buddha discovered, and what has been rediscovered by generation after generation of those who have practiced his teachings in their lives, is that there is a way to answer these difficult and wonderful questions. They are answered by an intuitive, silent knowing, by developing our own capacity to see clearly and directly.

How are we to begin? Traditionally, this understanding grows through the development of three aspects of our being: a ground of conscious conduct, a steadiness of the heart and mind, and a clarity of vision or wisdom.

Conscious Conduct: The Five Training Precepts

The first aspect, conscious conduct or virtue, means acting harmoniously and with care toward the life around us. For spiritual practice to develop, it is absolutely essential that we establish a basis of moral conduct in our lives. If we are engaged in actions that cause pain and conflict to ourselves and others, it is impossible for the mind to become settled, collected, and focused in meditation; it is impossible for the heart to open. To a mind grounded in unselfishness and truth, concentration and wisdom develop easily.

The Buddha outlined five areas of basic morality that lead to a conscious life. These training precepts are given to all students who wish to follow the path of mindfulness. They are not given as absolute commandments; rather, they are practical guidelines to help us live in a more harmonious way and develop peace and power of mind. As we work with them, we discover that they are universal precepts that apply to any culture, in any time. They are a part of basic mindfulness practice and can be cultivated in our spiritual life.

The first precept is to refrain from killing. It means honoring all life, not acting out of hatred or aversion in such a way as to cause harm to any living creature. We work to develop a reverence and caring for life in all its forms. In the Eightfold Path this is called one aspect of right action.

Even though it sounds obvious, we still manage to forget it. There was a cartoon in the *New Yorker* magazine some years ago during the hunting season. One deer turns to the other and says, "Why don't they thin their own goddamn herds?" We get into formulating excuses: "Well, there are too many deer." As we become more conscious and connected with life, it becomes clear that we shouldn't harm others, because it hurts us to kill. And they don't like it; even the tiniest creatures don't wish to die. So in practicing this precept we learn to stop creating pain for others and pain for ourselves.

The second precept asks us to refrain from stealing, meaning not to take what is not ours. Not to steal is called basic nonharming. We need to let go of being greedy and not take too much. More positively, it means to use things with sensitivity and care, to develop our sense of sharing this life, this planet. To live, we need plants, we need animals, and we need insects. This whole world has to share its resources. It is a boat of a certain size with so many beings living on it. We're connected with the bees and the insects and the earthworms. If there weren't earthworms to aerate the soil, and if there weren't bees to pollinate the crops, we'd starve. We need bees, we need insects. We're all interwoven. If we can learn to love the earth, we can be happy whatever we do, with a happiness born of contentment. This is the source of genuine ecology. It's a source of world peace, when we see that we're not separate from the earth but that we all come out of it and are connected with one another. From this sense of connectedness we can commit ourselves to share, to live a life of helpfulness and generosity for the world. To cultivate generosity directly is another fundamental part of living a spiritual life. Like the training precepts and like our inner meditations, generosity can actually be practiced. With practice, its spirit forms our actions, and our hearts will grow stronger and lighter. It can lead us to new levels of letting go and great happiness. The Buddha emphasized the importance of generosity when he said, "If you knew what I know about the power of giving, you would not let a single meal pass without sharing it in some way."

Traditionally there are described three kinds of giving, and we are encouraged to begin developing generosity at whatever level we find it arising in our heart. At first we find tentative giving. This is where we take an object and think, "Well, I'm probably not going to use this anyway. Maybe I should give it away. No, I should save it for next year. No, I'll give it away." Even this level is positive. It creates some joy for us and it helps someone else. It's a sharing and a connecting.

The next level of generosity to discover is friendly giving. It's like relating to a brother or sister. "Please share what I have; enjoy this as I do." Sharing openly of our time, our energy, the things we have, feels even better. It's lovely to do. The fact is that we do not need a lot of possessions to be happy. It is our relationship to this changing life that determines our happiness or sorrow. Happiness comes from the heart.

The third level of giving is kingly or queenly giving. It's where we take something—our time or our energy or an object that is the best we have—and give it to someone happily and say, "Please, would you enjoy this too." We give to the other person and take our joy in that sharing. This level of giving is a beautiful thing to learn.

As we start to learn to be more generous, to give more of our time, our energy, our goods, our money, we can find a way to do it not just to fit a self-image or please an external authority, but because it is a source of genuine happiness in our lives. Of course this doesn't mean giving everything away. That would be excessive, because we have to be compassionate and care for ourselves as well. Yet to understand the power of practicing this kind of openness is very special. It is a privilege to be able to bring this generosity into our lives.

The third precept of conscious conduct is to refrain from false speech. The Eightfold Path calls this right speech. Don't lie, it says. Speak only what is true and useful; speak wisely, responsibly, and appropriately. Right speech really poses a question.

It asks us to be aware of how we actually use the energy of our words. We spend so much of our lives talking and analyzing and discussing and gossiping and planning. Most of this talk is not very conscious or aware. It is possible to use speech to become awake. We can be mindful of what we are doing when we speak, of what the motivation is and how we are feeling. We can also be mindful in listening. We can align our speech to the principles of what is truthful and what is most kind or helpful. In practicing mindfulness we can begin to understand and discover the power of speech.

Once a master was called to heal a sick child with a few words of prayer. A skeptic in the crowd observed it all and expressed doubts about such a superficial way of healing. The master turned to him and said, "You know nothing of these matters; you are an ignorant fool!" The skeptic became very upset. He turned red and shook with anger. Before he could gather himself to reply, however, the master spoke again, asking, "When one word has the power to make you hot and angry, why should not another word have the power to heal?"

Our speech is powerful. It can be destructive and enlightening, idle gossip or compassionate communication. We are asked to be mindful and let our speech come from the heart. When we speak what is true and helpful, people are attracted to us. To be mindful and honest makes our minds quieter and more open, our hearts happier and more peaceful.

The fourth precept, to refrain from sexual misconduct, reminds us not to act out of sexual desire in such a way as to cause harm to another. It requires that we be responsible and honest in sexual relations. Sexual energy is very powerful. In these times of rapidly changing relationships and sexual values, we are asked to become conscious of our use of this power. If we associate this energy in our lives with grasping and greed, exploitation and compulsion, we will perform actions that bring harm to ourselves and others, such as adultery. There is great suffering consequent to these actions and great joy in the simplicity that comes in their absence.

The spirit of this precept asks us to look at the motivation behind our actions. To pay attention in this way allows us (as lay people) to discover how sexuality can be connected to the heart and how it can be an expression of love, caring, and genuine intimacy. We have almost all been fools at some time in our sexual life, and we have also used sex to try to touch what is beautiful, to touch another person deeply. Conscious sexuality is an essential part of living a mindful life.

To refrain from the heedless use of intoxicants is the fifth precept. It means to avoid taking intoxicants to the point of making the mind cloudy and to devote our lives instead to developing clarity and alertness. We have just one mind, so we must take care of it. In our country there are millions of alcoholics and others who have abused drugs. Their unconsciousness and fearful use of intoxicants has caused great pain to themselves, their families, and all those they touch. To live consciously is not easy—it means we often must face fears and pains that challenge our heart. Abuse of intoxicants is clearly not the way.

To enter the human realm, to establish a ground for spiritual life, requires that we bring awareness to all the actions in our world, to our use of intoxicants, our speech, to all of our actions. Establishing a virtuous and harmonious relationship to the world brings ease and lightness to the heart and steadfast clarity to the mind. A foundation of virtue brings great happiness and liberation in itself and is the precondition for wise meditation. With it we can be conscious and not waste the extraordinary opportunity of a human birth, the opportunity to grow in compassion and true understanding in our life.

Concentration of Mind

Out of a foundation of conscious conduct, the first steps of the mindful way, grows the second aspect of the path, which is called the development of samadhi, or steadiness and concentration of mind. As we bring the grace and harmony of virtue into our outer lives, so we can begin to establish an inner order, a sense of peace and clarity. This is the domain of formal meditation, and it begins with training the heart and mind in concentration. It means collecting the mind or bringing together the mind and body, focusing one's attention on one's experience in the present moment. Skill in concentrating and steadying the mind is the basis for all types of meditation and is in truth a basic skill for any endeavor, for art or athletics, computer programming or self-knowledge. In meditation, the development of the power of concentration comes through systematic training and can be done by using a variety of objects, such as the breath, visualization, a mantra, or a particular feeling such as loving kindness. We will speak much more fully about the art of concentrating the mind in later chapters, since it is so important. Most fundamentally it is a simple process of focusing and steadying attention on an object like the breath and bringing the mind back to that object again and again. It requires that we let go of thoughts about the past and future, of fantasies and attachment, and bring the mind back to what is actually happening; the actual moment of feeling, of touching the breath as it is. Samadhi doesn't just come of itself; it takes practice. What is wonderful is the discovery made by the Buddha and all great yogis that the mind can actually be trained.

There is a sign outside a casino in Las Vegas that says, "You must be present to win." The same is true in meditation. If we want to see the nature of our lives, we must actually be present, aware, awake. Developing samadhi is much like polishing a lens. If we are looking to see the cells and workings of the body with a lens that has not been ground sufficiently, we will not see clearly. In order to penetrate the nature of the mind and body, we must collect and concentrate our resources and observe with a steady, silent mind. This is exactly what the Buddha did: he sat, concentrated his mind, and looked within. To become a yogi, an explorer of the heart and mind, we must develop this capacity as well.

Wisdom

Built on the foundation of concentration is the third aspect of the Buddha's path of awakening: clarity of vision and the development of wisdom. In our lives there is much we don't see. We are too busy to see, or we forget or haven't learned about our capacity to see in new ways. Our steady and careful observation of the body, heart, and mind can bring about the growth of understanding and wisdom.

Wisdom comes from directly observing the truth of our experience. We learn as we become able to live fully in the moment, rather than being lost in the dreams, plans, memories, and commentaries of the thinking mind. There is a big difference between drinking a cup of tea while being there completely, and drinking a cup of tea while thinking about five other things. There is a big difference between taking a walk in the woods and really being there, and taking a walk and spending the whole time thinking about visiting Disneyland or what you are going to cook for dinner, or imagining all the stories you can tell your friends about what a great walk in the woods you had. It is only by being fully in the moment that the fundamental questions of the heart can be answered: it is only in the timeless moment that we can come to that intuitive, silent knowing of the truth. It is the intuitive wisdom that liberates us.

Inquiry and Observation

Wisdom grows out of our clear seeing in each moment. Seeing the arising and passing of our experience and how we relate to it. It arises through our gentle and careful inquiry into the workings of the body and mind and through an open inquiry into how this body and mind relate to the whole world around us. For insight to develop, this spirit of observation and deep questioning must be kept in the forefront. We can collect and quiet the mind, but then we must observe, examine, see its way and its laws.

As we meditate we can learn more about desire, see what its root is, see whether it is pleasant or painful, see how it arises and affects our life. We can equally well observe moments of stillness and contentment. We can also begin to observe the inner workings of cause and effect, the laws of karma. Similarly, the law of impermanence can reveal itself under our attention, how it operates, and whether there is anything in our experience that does not change. As things change, we can also observe how attachment works and see how tension and grasping are created in our body and mind. We can see what closes our heart, and how it can open. Over time we may discover new levels of stillness in ourselves or find lights or visions or a whole array of new inner experiences. We can also discover our shadow and bring our awareness to the fears and pains and deep feelings we have long suppressed in our lives. Insights about the psychological patterns we live by will arise, and we can see the functioning of the level we call the personality. When we bring the same spirit of inquiry and awareness to our relation with the whole world around us, our observation can also show us the illusions of our boundaries and how to truly connect the inner and the outer.

Beyond these, our inquiry can lead us to most fundamental spiritual questions, the nature of our own self. If everything we see is changing, what can we identify in this process as ourself? We can see what concepts or body image or deep sense of self we hold as "me" or "mine," as who we are, and begin to question this whole structure. And perhaps, in deep stillness, we can come to that which goes beyond our limited sense of self, that which is silent and timeless and universal.

Wisdom is not one particular experience, nor a series of ideas or knowledge to be collected. It is an ongoing process of discovery that unfolds when we live with balance and full awareness in each moment. It grows out of our sincerity and genuine openness, and it can lead us to a whole new world of freedom.

Insight meditation is a path of discovery. It is straightforward and direct, with no frills or gimmicks. It is simple, though not easy. Although the forms vary, the genuine practice of insight meditation is this single quest: to establish a foundation of harmonious action, to collect and concentrate the mind and body, and to see the laws of life by our own true, careful, and direct observation. After understanding the way of practice and realizing that meditative life involves this whole process of awakening, there is only one thing left to do. We have to undertake it ourselves.

J.K.

EXERCISE

Learning from the Precepts

Pick and refine one or more of the five basic training precepts as a way to cultivate and strengthen mindfulness. Work with a precept meticulously for one week. Then examine the results and choose another precept for a subsequent week. Here are some sample suggested ways to work with each precept.

1. *Refraining from killing: reverence for life.* Undertake for one week to purposefully bring no harm in thought, word, or deed to any living creature. Particularly become aware of any living beings in your world (people, animals, even plants) whom you ignore, and cultivate a sense of care and reverence for them too.

2. *Refraining from stealing: care with material goods.* Undertake for one week to act on every single thought of generosity that arises spontaneously in your heart.

3. *Refraining from false speech: speech from the heart.* Undertake for one week not to gossip (positively or negatively) or speak about anyone you know who is not present with you (any third party).

4. *Refraining from sexual misconduct: conscious sexuality.* Undertake for one week to

observe meticulously how often sexual feelings and thoughts arise in your consciousness. Each time, note what particular mind states you find associated with them, such as love, tension, compulsion, caring, loneliness, desire for communication, greed, pleasure, aggression, and so forth.

5. *Refraining from intoxicants to the point of heedlessness.* Undertake for one week or one month to refrain from all intoxicants and addictive substances (such as wine, marijuana, even cigarettes and/or caffeine if you wish). Observe the impulses to use these, and become aware of what is going on in the heart and mind at the time of those impulses.

2

MEDITATION INSTRUCTIONS

Keep your attention clearly focused on the sensations and feelings of each breath. Be with the breath at the place in the body where you feel it most clearly and distinctly—the rising and falling of the abdomen, the movement of the chest, or the in and out at the nostrils. See how carefully and continuously you can feel the sensations of the entire inhalation and exhalation, or the entire rising-and-falling movement.

Use a soft mental notation of "rise" and "fall" or "in" and "out" with each breath.

If there is a pause or space between the breaths, be aware of some touch point, either the buttocks on the cushion, the knees on the floor, or the lips as they gently touch each other, feeling accurately the particular sensations at that point. If there's a long pause between breaths, you can be aware of several touch sensations in succession until the next breath begins to come by itself, without hurrying or hastening the breathing process. When the next breath arrives, return the attention to the breathing, noting and noticing as carefully as possible.

Be aware and mindful of each breath, the rising and falling movement of the chest or abdomen, or the in and out of the air at the nostrils. Let the awareness be soft and relaxed, letting the breath come and go in its own rhythm. Feel the sensations of each breath accurately, not looking for anything in particular, but simply noticing what is actually there in each moment.

Sometimes the breath will be clear and sometimes indistinct, sometimes strong, sometimes very soft; it may be long or short, rough or smooth. Be with it as it reveals itself, aware of how it goes through various changes.

When sounds become predominant and call your attention away from the breathing, make a note of "hearing, hearing," focusing the attention and the awareness on the experience of the sound, not particularly getting involved in the concept of what's causing the sound, such as "car" or "wind," but just being with the vibration of hearing. See if you can experience the difference between the concept of the sound and the direct intuitive experience of it. Make a note of "hearing," and when it's no longer predominant or calling your attention, come back to the breath.

Often sounds will arise in the background of your awareness: that is, you are aware of them, but they're not particularly calling your attention away from the breath. In that case, there's no need to particularly make a mental note of "hearing." Simply stay with the noting of the breath, allowing the background awareness of sound simply to be there.

The continuity of attention and of mental noting strengthens the mindfulness and concentration. And so, with a gentleness of mind, make the effort to be as continuous in the noting as possible. When you go off, when you forget, when the mind wanders, make a note of "wandering" as soon as you're aware of it and come back to the breathing.

When sensations in the body become predominant and call your attention away from the breathing, focus all of the mindfulness, all of the attention onto that sensation itself. See how carefully you can observe and feel the quality of the sensation: is it hardness or softness, heat or cold, vibration, tingling, burning, pulling, tightness? Feel what the sensation is and notice as accurately as possible what happens to that sensation as you observe it. Does it get stronger, does it get weaker, does it dissolve, does it enlarge in size, does it get smaller?

Sometimes it may be difficult to find an exact word to describe the sensation. Don't spend much time thinking about it. If you can't find the right word intuitively in the moment, even a mental note of "sensation" or "feeling" will serve the purpose.

The awareness is most important. The noting is simply an aid in aiming the mind accurately toward the object in order to feel what the sensation is and to notice what happens to it as you observe it. For example, there may be a strong pain in the back or the knees. The mind attends to it, and it feels like burning. Notice that it's burning. As you watch it, you may notice that it gets stronger or weaker, expands in area or contracts. Sometimes it may disappear.

When the sensation is no longer predominant, return again to the in and out or rising and falling. Try to keep a balance in the mind of staying soft and relaxed, that quality of being settled back in the moment, and at the same time being alert and precise. Note carefully and gently moment after moment whatever object arises, coming back to the breath as the primary object when nothing else is predominant or calling the mind away.

Also notice any reactions in the mind to the different sensations. If you're observing painful feelings and you notice a reaction of aversion or restlessness or fear, make a note of those mind states, observing them carefully and seeing what happens to them as you note them. As you note "fear" or "aversion" or "restlessness," does it get stronger, does it get weaker, does it disappear? If you're observing pleasant sensations in the body and there's enjoyment or attachment, note that also.

There's no need to go looking for different objects. Keep the awareness very simple, staying grounded in the primary object of the breath, and then notice these different objects as they arise in their own time. The idea in practice is not to look for anything special and not to try to make anything special happen; rather it is to notice carefully what it is that is actually happening.

When thoughts arise in the mind, as soon as you become aware that you're thinking, make a soft mental note of "thinking" or "wandering." Sometimes you'll be aware of thoughts just in the moment of their arising, sometimes in the middle. Sometimes the mind won't be aware of a thought until it is completed. Notice when it is that you have become aware of thinking, without judgment or evaluation. At whatever point the mind becomes aware, make the note of "thinking" and then gently come back to the breathing. There need not be any struggle or conflict with the thought process; simply note it at whatever point you become aware.

Likewise, if images or pictures arise in the mind, make a note of "seeing"; if sounds become predominant, make a note of "hearing." Let the awareness come out of a receptivity of mind, settling back in a soft and open way. As different objects of experience reveal themselves, be mindful and attentive to each object, and notice what happens to it as it is observed.

Sometimes the mind may get confused by too many objects or isn't clearly aware of where to focus. At that time make a note of that kind of confusion or uncertainty and return to the breath as an anchor. The breathing is useful as the primary object because for the most part it's always present. So one can always come back to the breath, settling into it, feeling it, noticing it. When the mind feels centered with the breathing, again notice the different objects that may arise.

When different mind states and emotions become predominant, they too should be made the object of awareness. If we're not aware of them when they arise, they become unconscious filters on our experience and we begin to view everything through the filter of a particular emotion. Sometimes they may come associated with thoughts or images or with certain sensations in the body. There may be feelings of happiness or sadness, frustration, anger, annoyance, joy, interest, excitement, restlessness, or fear. Many different kinds of mind states may arise.

As soon as you become aware that some mind state or emotion or mood is in the mind, make a specific note of that particular state of mind, so as not to get lost in it and not to be identified with it. These mind states, like all other objects, are arising and passing away. They are not "I," not self, and do not belong to anyone. Note the mind state, be open to the experience of it, and when it's no longer predominant, return to the breath or to sensations in the body.

Be particularly vigilant with respect to the arising of the five hindrances: desire, aversion, sleepiness, restlessness, and doubt. These are strongly conditioned in the mind, and it is easy to get lost in and become identified with them. Make a special effort to notice these particular mind states. The more quickly they can be observed, as close to the beginning as possible, the less their power will be.

In addition to paying attention to the breath, sensations, sounds, thoughts, images, emotions, and mind states, there is one more factor of mind that is important to single out and notice carefully in the meditation practice, because it plays a very critical role in opening the doors of deeper insight. That is becoming aware of and noting the various intentions in the mind. Intention is that mental factor or mental quality that directly precedes a bodily action or movement.

The body by itself doesn't move. It moves as the result of a certain impulse or volition. So before beginning any movement of the body, notice the intention to move, the intention to stand, the intention to shift position, the intention to turn, the intention to reach.

Before each of these movements there will be a volition in the mind. Intention or volition is quite subtle. It's not a tangible, discrete object like a thought or an image that you can see clearly having a beginning, middle, and end. At first the intention might be experienced simply as a pause before the movement begins, a moment's pause in which you know that you are about to do something. If you acknowledge the pause and make the note "intending," that will serve the purpose.

It is important to begin to be aware of these intentions, for two reasons. First, it illuminates and reveals the cause-and-effect relationship between mind and body. This is one of the fundamental laws that leads to deeper understanding. The unfolding of the process of mind and body is happening lawfully, and one of the laws that describes this process is the law of cause and effect. By noting "intention," we get a preliminary understanding of how this works. Because of an intention, the body moves. Intention is the cause; movement is the effect. As we note it in our experience, it becomes increasingly clear.

Noting "intention" also helps us to discover and understand the selfless nature of the mind-body process. Even when we are observing the breath, sensations, thoughts, images, and emotions, and we begin to see that all of these objects are simply part of a passing show, we may still be identified with the sense of a doer, the director of it all, the one who is commanding the actions.

When we note intentions and see that they are also passing mental phenomena, that they arise and pass away, that intentions themselves are not "I" and not "mine," when we see that they do not belong to anybody, we begin to loosen the sense of identification with them. We experience on deeper and deeper levels the selflessness of the whole unfolding process.

We begin with the breath, opening to the feeling or the sensation of each breath, each movement of the rise and fall or in and out, without any expectation of how any particular breath should be, not trying to force it into a particular pattern, not thinking that there should be any one kind of sensation. It is a settling back into each moment, with a great deal of care and precision, and being open to what is revealed in that particular breath. What is the sensation of this rising, or this in-breath? What is the feeling of it? Is it long or short, is it rough or smooth, is it deep or shallow, is there heaviness or pressure or tingling?

There is no need to go through a checklist. Just by our being open and paying careful attention, the characteristics of each breath will show themselves. So we settle back and stay open, with a beginner's mind for each rising, each falling, each in-breath, each out-breath.

If there is a space or a pause between the breaths, notice one or more touch-points, making the note "touching, touching." When sensations in the body become predominant, when they're calling the attention away from the breathing, let the mind go to the sensation that is predominant; open to it, feel it. Note what kind of sensation it is. Is it heat or cold, heaviness or lightness, is it vibration or tingling, is it a painful sensation or a pleasant one?

When you open with awareness to each sensation, the characteristics of that sensation will become obvious. Let the mind stay very receptive to the sensations. Note what happens as you observe them. Do they get stronger, do they get weaker, do they disappear, do they increase? Observe what happens, without any model or expectation of what should be there; simply be with what is. When the sensations are no longer predominant, return again to the breath.

Keep a sense of alertness in the mind with respect to different mental phenomena, noting "thinking" or "seeing" as soon as you become aware that a thought or image is present. Observe what happens to that thought or image when you note it. Does it continue or does it disappear? If it disappears, does it disappear quickly or slowly? When a thought or image is no longer predominant, return to the awareness of the breath. Keep this movement from object to object fluid, rhythmic, and relaxed. There's no need to go searching for particular objects; rather, maintain a quality of openness and alertness so that whatever presents itself becomes the object of awareness, and let all objects of body and mind arise and pass away by themselves. Our practice is simply to settle back and note in each moment what is arising, without judgment, without evaluation, without interpretation. It is simple, bare attention to what is happening.

Stay mindful too of the different mind states or emotions. These states are less clearly defined as objects. They don't have such a clear beginning, middle, and end, and yet they can become very predominant objects of experience. So if a mind state or emotion or mood becomes strong—feelings such as sadness or happiness or anger or desire, restlessness or excitement, interest or rapture, joy or calm—make the mental note of that mind state, feeling it and observing how that too is a part of the passing show. It arises, it is there for some time, it passes away.

Use the breathing as a primary object,

being with it if nothing else is very predominant and coming back to the breath when other objects disappear. Also, if the mind is feeling scattered or confused, without knowing exactly what to observe, center the attention on the breathing, either the rise and fall or in and out. When the mind feels more centered and steady, again open the awareness to the entire range of changing objects—the breath, sounds, sensations, thoughts, images, intentions, emotions—noting each in turn as they arise. Keep the mind open, receptive, and alert, so that in each moment there can be an accurate awareness of what is present.

J.G.

3

DIFFICULTIES AND HINDRANCES

THE BUDDHIST TRADITION speaks directly about the hindrances that are encountered in the course of the spiritual journey. Buddha said that those who conquer their own minds are greater than those who defeat a thousand men a thousand times in battle. Almost every experienced yogi can describe in detail hours or years of dealing with some version of the five basic hindrances, the disruptions of mind and blocks to the heart that arise in practice. These same difficult energies are equally well described by Christian and

Jewish mystics, Sufis, Hindu yogis, and American Indian shamans.

There is a story told of Mother Teresa of Calcutta. After praising her extraordinary work, an interviewer for the BBC remarked that in some ways service might be a bit easier for Mother Teresa than for us ordinary householders. After all, she has no possessions, no car, no insurance, and no husband. "This is not true," she replied at once. "I am married too." She held up the ring that nuns in her order wear to symbolize their wedding to Christ. Then she added, "And he can be very difficult sometimes!" The hindrances and difficulties in spiritual practice are universal.

When we examine our own minds we will inevitably encounter the root forces of greed, fear, prejudice, hatred, and desire, which create so much sorrow in the world. They become an opportunity for us. They raise a central question for anyone who undertakes a spiritual life. Is there some way that we can live with these forces constructively and wisely? Is there a skillful way to work with these energies? These are not just contemporary problems. In the second century Evagrios, one of the Christian mystics known as the desert fathers, taught his students about the hindrances by describing them in terms of demons that come to one who meditates out in the wilderness. The demons include fear, irritation, gluttony, laziness, and pride. In the Buddhist tradition, they are personified by Mara, the Tempter. They are our fear, our habits, our anger, our resistance, our unwillingness to look at what is actually happening.

As we meditate, Mara comes in many forms. First it may come as temptation and desire, as fantasy, as looking for comfort; Mara is all the things that say, "Let's do this instead." If the temptations don't work and we are still willing to continue, Mara comes to us in a more ferocious guise. It comes as an attacker, as anger, irritability, or doubt. And if we are unmoved by Mara as tempter or attacker, then Mara comes in yet a more subtle form. It comes with whispers of pride; "Oh, look, how good I am! I didn't give in to the temptation" or "I've gotten rid of the anger." Things become a little clear, and we settle for that. We get caught trying to hold on to our concentration and stillness or some particular meditative state.

When the Buddha sat under the bodhi tree, he vowed not to get up until he had come to the fullest understanding and freedom possible for a human. To understand the nature of happiness and sorrow, to find freedom in our life, we have to be willing to face all the demons in our mind. Our journey—our practice through all the realms of our mind—is to learn a kind of mind control, a traveler's equilibrium. It is not the control of making something happen, but rather the ability to stay present, open, and balanced through all the experiences and realms of life. Through practice it is possible to train the heart and mind, to make them concentrated, to make them steady and luminous and free. It's possible to become balanced in the face of every kind of experience. Ultimately, it is possible to overcome and transform the forces of Mara with the sincerity of our practice, which means our love and the willingness to be truly mindful. With honesty we can learn to be unmoved. We can come to understand that which is deeper than those forces. We start to see that the worst and most difficult things also change, that they too are empty experiences, light and shadows that we all share and that arise and pass in the clear space of mind.

The beauty of these teachings is that

they are not just theoretical or grandiose. There is a practical path we can follow to experience whole new levels of happiness in our lives, to learn a new relationship with ourselves and our experience. Depending on our relationship to these hindrances, they can be the cause of tremendous struggle or valuable fuel for the growth of insight. The first step necessary in working with these energies is to identify them clearly. Classically, there are said to be five primary hindrances, although you may have discovered some of your own. In fact, many yogis speak of being assailed by several of them at once—the "multiple-hindrance attack." To understand them better, let us consider them one at a time.

The Five Hindrances

The first hindrance is desire for sense pleasure: pleasant sights, sounds, smells, tastes, bodily sensations, and mind states. What's the problem with desire—what's wrong with it? Nothing, really. There's nothing wrong with enjoying pleasant experiences. Given the difficulties we face in life, they are nice to have. But they fool us. They trick us into adopting the "if only" mentality: "If only I could have this," or "If only I had the right job," or "If only I could find the right relationship," or "If only I had the right clothes," or "If only I had the right personality, then I would be happy." We are taught that if we can get enough pleasurable experiences, pasting them together quickly one after another, our life will be happy. A good game of tennis followed by a delicious dinner, a fine movie, then wonderful sex and sleep, a good morning jog, a fine hour of meditation, an excellent breakfast, and off to an exciting morning at work, and so on. Our society is masterful at perpetuating the ruse: "Buy this, look like that, eat that, act like this, own that . . . and you too can be happy." There is no problem with enjoying pleasant experiences, and to practice does not mean to dismiss them. But they don't really satisfy the heart, do they? For a moment we experience a pleasant thought or taste or sensation, and then it's gone, and with it the sense of happiness it brought. Then it's on to the next thing. The whole process can become very tiring and empty.

Of course we don't always ask for a lot; sometimes we settle for very little. At the beginning of a meditation retreat people often spend a lot of time dwelling on desires they carry in with them: "If only I had that house," or "If only I had more money." But as they settle into the limits placed on them by the retreat, the desires get smaller: "If only they would put out something sweet after lunch," or "If only the sitting were five minutes shorter." In a situation like a retreat—or a prison, for that matter—where the possibilities for fulfilling desires are limited, it becomes clear that the strength of a desire is determined not by the particular object, but by the degree of attachment in the mind, and the desire for a piece of candy can be as powerful as the desire for a Mercedes Benz.

Again, the problem is not the object of desire, but the energy in the mind. The energy of desire keeps us moving, looking for that thing that is really going to do it for us. The wanting mind is itself painful. It's a self-perpetuating habit that does not allow us to be where we are because we are grasping for something somewhere else. Even when we get what we want, we then want something more or different because the habit of wanting is so strong. It is a sense that being here and now is not enough, that we are somehow incomplete, and it keeps us cut off from the joy of our own natural completeness. We are never content. It is the same force in the world at large that creates the havoc of people wanting and consuming, hoarding, and fighting wars to have more and more, for pleasure and for security that are never fulfilled.

In India they say that when a pickpocket meets a saint, the pickpocket sees only the saint's pockets. What we want will distort and limit our perception; it will determine what we see. If we are hungry and we walk down the street, we don't see shoe stores or the weather or the clouds. We see there is a nice Greek restaurant. "I could have feta cheese and a nice salad," or "There's an Italian restaurant. Maybe I'll have pizza or manicotti," or "There's McDonald's. Maybe I'll have a burger."

People can get so lost in the imagination that meditators on retreat have often glimpsed a potential partner and gone through a whole romance (meeting, courtship, marriage, children, even divorce) without ever actually saying a word to that person. We call this the vipassana romance.

So the force of desire can cloud our minds, bringing distortion and delusion in its wake. As it says in the *Tao Te Ching*, "The secret waits for eyes unclouded by longing." We can see how desire interferes with our being able to open up to things as they are, in a freer, more joyful way. It interferes with our power to deeply open to the truth, to relate directly and wisely to what is actually here.

The second difficult energy we encounter is aversion, hatred, anger, and ill will. While desire and the wanting mind are seductive and can easily fool us, the opposite energy of anger and aversion is clearer because its unpleasantness is obvious. Anger and hatred are usually painful. We might find some enjoyment in it for a while, but it closes our heart. It has a burning, tight quality that we can't get away from.

Like desire, anger is an extremely powerful force. It can be experienced toward an object that is present with us or one that is far away. We sometimes experience great anger over past events that are long gone and about which we can do nothing. Strangely enough, we can even get furious over something that has not happened, but that we only imagine might. When it is strong in the mind, anger colors our entire experience of life. When our mood is bad, then no matter who walks in the room or where we go that day, something is wrong. Anger can be a source of tremendous suffering in our own minds, in our interactions with others, and in the world at large.

Although we generally don't think of them as such, fear and judgment and boredom are all forms of aversion. When we examine them, we see that they are based on our dislike of some aspect of experience. With the mind full of dislike, full of wanting to separate or withdraw from our experience, how can we become concentrated or explore the present moment in a spirit of discovery? To practice we need to come very close to and investigate this moment, not push it away or pull away from it. So we need to learn to work with all these forms of our aversion.

The third common hindrance that arises is sloth and torpor. This includes laziness, dullness, lack of vitality, fogginess, and sleepiness. Clarity and wakefulness fade when the mind is overcome with sloth and torpor. The mind becomes unworkable and cloudy. When sloth and torpor overcome us, it is a big obstacle in practice.

Restlessness, the opposite of torpor,

manifests as the fourth hindrance. With restlessness there is agitation, nervousness, anxiety, and worry. The mind spins in circles or flops around like a fish out of water. The body can be filled with restless energy, vibrating, jumpy, on edge. Or sometimes we sit down to meditate and the mind runs through the same routines over and over. Of course, no matter how much we worry and fret over something, it never helps the situation. Still the mind gets caught in reminiscences and regrets, and we spin out hours of stories. When the mind is restless, we jump from object to object. It is difficult to sit still, and our concentration becomes scattered and dispersed.

The last of the five hindrances is doubt. Doubt can be the most difficult of all to work with, because when we believe it and get caught by it, our practice just stops cold. We become paralyzed. All kinds of doubt might assail us; doubts about ourselves and our capacities, doubts about our teachers, doubts about the dharma itself—"Does it really work? I sit here and all that happens is my knees hurt and I feel restless. Maybe the Buddha really didn't know what he was talking about." We might doubt the practice or doubt that it is the right practice for us. "It's too hard. Maybe I should try Sufi dancing." Or we think it's the right practice but the wrong time. Or it's the right practice and the right time, but our body's not yet in good enough shape. It doesn't matter what the object is; when the skeptical, doubting mind catches us, we're stuck.

Working with the Hindrances

How do these five hindrances interfere with our clarity of mind? There is a traditional analogy comparing our nature to a pond, and the point of practice is to see to the depths of the pond. Desire comes like beautifully colored dyes in the water that obstruct our vision. When we are angry it is as though the pond were on a boiling-hot spring. Again, we cannot see far. Sloth and torpor are like a thick layer of algae growing on the pond's surface. Restlessness is like a strong wind blowing on the pond's surface and creating waves. And doubt is like mud stirred up from the pond's bottom. Getting caught by any of these hindrances makes it impossible to see clearly into our heart and mind.

We are each challenged by these hindrances again and again in the course of our practice. So it is important that we learn to work with them when they arise. If we are able to work with them skillfully, we can actually use these times to strengthen, clarify, and deepen our awareness and understanding.

How do we approach them? Certainly

not by judgment or suppression. Suppression doesn't work, because suppression is itself a form of aversion. It deadens our awareness and our life. On the other hand, we don't want to get involved in expressing all the hindrances and acting them all out. That simply reinforces the patterns (and might get us in other trouble as well).

If we don't suppress these energies and don't act upon all of them, then what is left? The most direct way is to be mindful of them, to transform them into the object of meditation. Through the power of mindfulness we can make these very forces another aspect of our meditation, using awareness of them to bring the mind to greater freedom. Working with them can be the source of insight and energy. We can directly observe the nature of desire, anger, doubt, and fear and really understand how these forces operate in the mind. We can use their power to enliven and strengthen our investigation. And these very forces can teach us the truth of the dharma, for we can see in their operation the laws of karma, or impermanence and impersonality. With mindfulness, our way of transforming Mara's army is wonderfully simple. We don't have to fight to overcome them. Instead, through awareness, we allow their energy to teach us their laws. We learn to experience even their extremes without being caught or overcome by them. Learning to work with the hindrances in this way is a particularly important part of actualizing our practice amid the stress and demands of daily life.

There is a second whole way of working with hindrances. This is recommended for use when they are particularly strong. Through cultivating their opposite states as a balance or remedy, we can help weaken the hindrances and unhook ourselves from our strong entanglement with them. When they are weaker, we are better able to observe them mindfully. A third way for more advanced students to work with these energies deserves a brief mention as well. When concentration becomes quite strong and the power of mindfulness is well developed, it becomes possible to simply *let go* of these states as soon as they arise. This letting go has no aversion in it; it is a directed choice to abandon one mind state and redirect the concentration to a more skillful object such as the breath or a state of mental calm. This ability will come spontaneously in deeper states of practice, and most students need not be concerned with it unless it arises naturally. It cannot be used in the early parts of practice because without sufficient balance and steadiness it easily becomes aversion, a movement of judgment to get rid of the hindrances instead of observing them with mindfulness.

Let us begin with our usual meditations. How do we actually apply these ways of working in practice? For example, if sense desire arises, greed arises, wanting arises, what do we do? We look directly at this mind state and include it in the field of awareness. First make a soft mental note of it: "desire, desire." We can observe sense desire just as we observe the breath or sensations in the body. When a strong desire arises, turn all the attention to it; see it clearly. What is this desire? How does it feel in the body? What parts of the body are affected by it—the gut, the breath, the eyes? What does it feel like in the heart, in the mind? When it is present, are we happy or agitated, open or closed? Note "desire, desire" and see what happens to it. Pay meticulous attention.

If we look closely, we can learn a lot about this force that so greatly affects our lives and the world around us. It can cause wars; it is the force behind all the advertising in our society, behind much of our life. Have we ever stopped to examine it, to feel it directly, to discover a wise relation to it? When we look, we see that it creates tension, that it is actually painful. We can see how it arises out of our sense of longing and incompleteness, the feeling that we are separate and not whole. We see that it is also impermanent, essenceless. As we investigate desire, it reveals itself to us. It is actually just a thought and an accompanying feeling that comes and goes from the empty mind—that is all it is. That is easy to notice when we are not caught up in it, but many other times it seems very real. As Oscar Wilde said, "I can resist anything but temptation." The wanting mind is powerful, and learning to observe it will take some practice. Much of the power of desire comes from its being a habit with us. Our habitual patterns of desire are conditioned and reinforced in many ways, and they have tremendous momentum. But being mindful of desire does not mean getting involved in aversion toward it. Rather, it means watching desire come and go without being caught by it, and seeing its nature clearly.

Still, many times as we look carefully we can also see that beneath desire there is a more neutral, universal energy with which we live, an energy called the will to do. While sometimes it is associated with greed and grasping, it can also be directed by love, by compassion, and by wisdom. With the development of awareness we can get a taste of living in states free from so much desire, of a more spontaneous and natural way of being without as much struggle or ambition. When we are no longer caught by desire, compassion and understanding will more naturally direct our life. This can be experienced and sensed directly in our practice. But it cannot be grasped by our thinking mind. It comes more clearly as we begin to recognize the moments of desirelessness and contentment that come between our desires. This is an exquisite area in which to pay attention.

When desire arises, it is a force that pulls us out of the moment into our imagination. Sometimes it becomes so strong that we are unable to watch it. One antidote is to resolve to practice moderation with regard to the object of desire. Another antidote is to reflect on impermanence, even on death. How much will fulfilling this desire mean at the end of our life? Recognize that no matter how many times we get what we want, it always passes. It's endless. It's like one of the Sufi tales about Mullah Nasruddin. After buying a basket of hot chili peppers because they were so cheap he couldn't resist, he began to eat them. Tears streamed down his cheeks, his tongue burned, and yet he continued. When one of his students asked him why, he replied, "I keep waiting for a sweet one!"

Of course, in our lives we will still act on desire much of the time. If we become mindful of it, then even our action will teach us, instead of just reinforcing our habits. One Indian meditation teacher who had a powerful craving for sweets tried to let go of it in sitting without much success. So one day he went out and bought a huge plate of his favorite sugary sweets. He planned to eat the whole thing, trying to be mindful as he did so. Actually he could hardly begin. By the end of that plate he was sick of sweets and a lot freer of the desire. But we have to pay attention to learn. When desire arises, look at it and let it come and go of itself. If it is too strong and you are unable to be mindful of it, use a remedy to help bring the mind back to balance. But continue to pay attention. It is making these energies mindful that brings insight and wisdom in our practice.

How can we work with the opposite of desire, aversion? Again, we begin by making the effort to be mindful of it, experiencing it fully and noting it as "anger, anger." Anger presents us with the same opportunity to learn, to find greater freedom. So we should not fear it, but investigate it. How does anger feel? Where in the body do we feel it? What is its temperature, its effect on the breath, its degree of pain? How does it affect the mind? Is the mind smaller, more rigid, tighter? We can learn a lot from anger. Anger shows us precisely where we are stuck, where our limits are, where we cling to beliefs and fears. Aversion is like a warning signal lighting up and saying "attached, attached." The amount of attachment is revealed by the strength of our anger. Often we cannot change the conditions of our life, but we can always learn from them. Here, anger has come to teach us about its true nature, and our attention shows us the hurt, attachment, and identification that underlie it. Yet the attachment is optional. We can relate more wisely. When we stop and look at it, we will discover something fundamental about anger: conditioned by our viewpoint on that day, it is impermanent. It's a feeling with associated sensations and thoughts that come and go. We do not need to be bound to it or driven by it.

Of course, many of us have been conditioned to hate our anger. As we try to observe it, we will find a tendency to judge and suppress it—to get rid of it because it is "bad" and painful, or shameful and unspiritual. We must be very careful to bring an open mind and heart to our mindfulness. We need to let ourselves feel fully, even if it means touching the deepest wells of grief, sorrow, and rage within us. These are the forces that move our lives, and these are what we must feel and come to terms with. It's not a process of getting rid of something, but one of opening and understanding. So when anger or irritation or fear or boredom arises—any of these states rooted in aversion to experience—we must explore and observe it fully. We may need to actually let ourselves get caught up in it sometimes to understand it well. We will probably note anger or fear arising many times in practice before we have come to a balanced, mindful way. This is natural.

What we have to understand in working with anger and ill will is true of all the difficulties in our practice: that they are our strongest teachers. This became very clear in the spiritual community that G. I.

Gurdjieff led in France. One old man who lived there was the personification of these qualities—irritable, messy, fighting with everyone, and unwilling to clean up or help at all. No one got along with him. Finally, after many frustrating months of trying to stay with the group, the old man left for Paris. Gurdjieff followed him and tried to convince him to return, but it had been too hard, and the man said no. At last Gurdjieff offered the man a very big monthly stipend if he returned. How could he refuse? When he returned everyone was aghast, and on hearing that he was being paid (while they were being charged a lot to be there), the community was up in arms. Gurdjieff called them together and after hearing their complaints laughed and explained: "This man is like yeast for bread." He said, "Without him here you would never really learn about anger, irritability, patience, and compassion. That is why you pay me, and why I hire him."

All these forces are part of our practice. Our main tool is to examine them with mindfulness. Still there are times when hatred and anger are too strong to watch. We can often balance them by developing thoughts of compassion and forgiveness. This is not just a papering over of anger; it is a deep movement of the heart, a willingness to go beyond the conditions of a particular point of view. When we feel anger toward someone, we can consider that he or she is a being just like us, who has faced much suffering in life. If we had experienced the same circumstances and history of suffering as the other person, might we not act in the same way? So we allow ourselves to feel compassion, to feel his or her suffering. We can also first reflect upon someone we love very much and let loving thoughts grow in our heart, and then extend that energy toward the person or situation that is the object of our hatred. In this way, we do not cut off from the power of love and compassion within us. It is a very real power and an accessible one when we can remember it, and we can use it to still the turbulence and confusion that often surrounds our anger.

Boredom, judgment, and fear are also forms of aversion that we can learn to be mindful of. Usually we are afraid of boredom and will do anything to avoid it. So we go to the refrigerator, pick up the phone, watch TV, read a novel, busy ourselves constantly to escape our loneliness, our emptiness, our boredom. Without awareness it has a great power over us. Yet we need not let boredom run our lives this way. What is boredom when it is experienced in itself? Have we ever really stopped to look at it? Boredom comes from lack of attention. With it we also find restlessness, discouragement, and judgment. We get bored because we don't like what is happening and so don't pay attention. But if we stay with it, a whole new level of understanding and contentment can grow. In meditation we let boredom itself be an object of interest to explore. When it arises, feel the boredom. Note it, feel its texture, its energy, the pains and tension in it, the resistances to it. Look directly at the workings of this quality in the body and mind. We can finally stop running away or resisting it. Insight, consciousness, freedom are to be found not in some other experience, in some other moment, but in any moment in which we really learn to pay attention. When the awareness is clear and focused, even the repeated movement of the in- and out-breath can be the most incredibly interesting and wonderful experience.

In the same way, we can become aware

of judgment. If we observe, we can see that judgment is actually just a thought, a series of words in the mind. When we don't get caught up in the story line, we can learn a great deal about the nature of thought by watching the judging mind. We can learn a great deal about the nature of suffering in life as well. Start by simply noting "judging" when it arises—and noting it softly, like a whisper, not like a baseball bat, trying to get rid of it, because that's just more judging! At times in practice we find how incredibly active the judging mind is. We judge everything: too noisy, too fast, too hard, too long, too much, too little. This is bad, that's no good, and underneath, fundamentally, we ourselves are judged as not being good. It is helpful to bring a lightness and tenderness to observing this aspect of mind. For humor, we can also count the judgments, like counting sheep. See if it is possible to discover 300 subtle judgments in an hour of sitting. This can bring a tremendous leap in attention.

Fear will also come in practice. It comes strongly for everyone at certain times. Let yourself experience it mindfully, noting, "fear, fear, fear." How does it feel? Where do you feel it in the body? What is it like in the heart, the mind? Of course, there are times when we are really caught by it. We identify with it, we resist it and push it away. To work with it mindfully, we must soften the attention and let ourselves touch it with our heart. Try not to be afraid of it. Sit with it, be aware of it, and after much practice, at some point there will simply come the recognition, "Oh, fear. Here you are again. Now, that's interesting." We will have made friends with our fear.

As our capacity to be mindful grows more continuous, we can find ourselves filled with joy and rapture. These states are born out of wholehearted attention and deep interest in the present moment. The fullness of our being is what provides this joy, not the particular object of the moment. A sight, a sound, a taste—whatever it is, it is not the source. When this unique kind of joy is present, anger and fear have ceased to overpower us, and we can taste another level of freedom.

Sloth and torpor are the next difficult energy. Sleepiness has three causes. One is the tiredness that signals a genuine need for sleep. This often comes in the first few days of a retreat or at home after a long day, when we sit after a period of great business and stress. This kind of sleepiness passes after we take some rest. The second kind of sleepiness comes as resistance to some unpleasant or fearful state of body or mind. We don't want to feel something, and so we get sleepy. A third cause of sleepiness is a result of the imbalance of concentration and energy in practice.

Usually sleepiness comes upon us gradually. As we sit, we can feel the sleepiness begin like tendrils of fog curling around our body and then whispering in our ear. "Come on, let's just take a little snooze. It'll be really nice." The mind then becomes dissipated and depleted, and we lose heart for what we have undertaken. This can happen many times in our sittings. Yet sleepiness is a workable state. To practice with sleepiness requires our full endeavor, because it is a powerful condition. Much of living is only half awake. Our life has been spent in sleep and sleepwalking; meditation means waking up. So we being by noting it and bringing mindfulness to the sleepiness. Be aware of how the body feels when it's tired, the heaviness, the softening posture, the sense in the eyes. Of course, if we're sleepy and nodding off, it is somewhat difficult to watch. Observe as much as you are able. Pay attention to its beginning, middle, and end, and to the various components of the experience. See the impersonal conditions that cause it. Is it tiredness or resistance? Sometimes interested, penetrating awareness of sleepiness can itself arouse the energy to dispel the sleepiness and bring insight and understanding. Sometimes when we recognize that the sleepy or lazy mind is resistance in us, we can discover an important fear or difficulty just underneath it. Such states as loneliness, sorrow, emptiness, and loss of control are common ones that we avoid, and when we recognize them with mindfulness, our whole practice can open up to a new level. It is useful to know that some sleepiness can also be caused by the development of concentration and calm in the mind. If we get quite concentrated but have not balanced the mind by arousing an equal amount of energy, we will be stuck in a calm but dull state. This, too, requires careful attention.

There are other ways of working with this hindrance. Sit up straight and take a few deep breaths. Meditate with your eyes open wide. Stand in place for a few minutes or do walking meditation. If it's really bad, walk briskly or walk backward. Splash some water on your face. Sleepiness is something we can respond to creatively. When I was going through a long period of sleepiness in practice, my teacher, Achaan Chaa, had me sit on the edge of a very deep well. The fear of falling in kept me quite awake! Sleepiness is workable. When the mind is attacked by sluggishness and it becomes too constricted and heavy, our effort should be to balance the mind by making it more alive. We can accomplish this through continually trying to direct the mind to the object of this very moment, and then this very moment, and so on. The accuracy and immediacy of the watchfulness—saying in effect, "Just this breath" or "Just this step," without trying to see beyond it, will steady the mind. If we can say, "Just this breath," in every single moment, from moment to moment, the mind will become expansive and refreshed, and sluggishness will disappear. When nothing at all seems to work, then it is time to rest.

The fourth common difficult energy is restlessness. When this comes on the inner radio, try not to judge it or condemn it. Like all other phenomena, it is conditioned and it comes and goes. Be mindful and note, "restless, restless." Let yourself experience restlessness without indulging or getting caught up in the content of its story. It can be terribly unpleasant; the body filled with nervous energy, the mind spinning with worry. Open to it and observe it without identifying with it or taking it as self. It is not "my restlessness," but rather an impermanent state born out of conditions and bound to change. If it gets very intense, think to yourself, "Okay, I'm ready. I'll be the first meditator in America to actually die of restlessness." Surrender and see what happens. Like everything else, restlessness is a composite, a series of thoughts, feelings, and sensations. But because we believe it to be something solid, it has a great deal of power over us. When we stop resisting and simply allow it to move through us with mindful attention, we can see how transitory and insubstantial the state actually is.

One antidote to restlessness is concentration. When restlessness is too strong to simply observe, try relaxing and counting your breaths—one to ten, then start again at one—until the mind comes back to balance. If it helps, breathe slightly more deeply than usual as a way of collecting and softening the body and mind.

Part of understanding restlessness is understanding that meditation, like life, has its way of recycling. Some people don't like the aspect of life that has so many cycles. They want it to be very even and not have so many ups and downs. Unfortunately, on our planet, things don't work that way. There are constant changes. Our practice is to relate to what Zorba the Greek called "the whole catastrophe," all the parts of it—the beautiful, the pleasant, the troublesome, and the unpleasant—with a certain amount of ease and humor.

This quality of acceptance is the ground out of which true insight and understanding develop. If we don't accept some aspect of ourselves—a feeling, a physical or mental sense of ourselves—then we cannot learn about it. We cannot discover its nature and become free in relationship to it. We become afraid, we resist, we judge, and we try to push away. We cannot look deeply and push away at the same time. When mindfulness is well developed and the ground of acceptance is laid, then the body and mind are filled with a sense of comfort. Even if something difficult or painful has arisen, this comfort is underlying it. The element of comfort is also an antidote to restlessness and anxiety.

The fifth hindrance is doubt. Look at it carefully and with detachment. Have we ever really observed the voice that says, "I can't do it. It's too hard. It's the wrong time to sit. Where is this getting me anyway? Maybe I should try some other practice"? What do we see? Doubt is a string of words in the mind, often associated with a subtle feeling of fear and resistance. When we become mindful of doubt as a thought process, when we note, "doubting, doubting," and when we do not become involved in its content, a marvelous transformation occurs: doubt itself becomes the source of awareness. We can learn a great deal about the impermanent, ungraspable nature of the mind through watching doubt. We also learn about what it means to be identified with and caught up in our moods and state of mind. When we are caught up in doubt, there is a great deal of suffering. And in the moment, when we feel it without grasping, our whole mind becomes freer and lighter.

One aspect of doubt that is especially difficult is the inability of the mind to focus on anything; the mind runs all over the place, considering possibilities, and remains indecisive. An antidote to this is to come fully back to the present moment, with a degree of continuity, a firmness and steadiness of mind. Gradually, this dispels confusion. Sometimes doubt is too strong, and we become muddled in it. Doubt can be balanced by developing faith. To strengthen faith we can ask questions or read great books. We can reflect on the inspiration of the hundreds of thousands of people in the spiritual life who have followed the path of inner awareness and practice before us. It has been valued by every great culture. To live with great wisdom and compassion is possible for anyone who genuinely undertakes a training of their heart and mind. What better thing to do with our life? A clear understanding of the teachings and wise reflecting upon them can inspire faith and help the mind return to a place of balance. It is natural for the heart to doubt. But let us understand it and let the doubt lead us to a deeper attention and a more complete seeking for the truth.

All of the kinds of doubts that come as a resistance—"It's not working today, I'm not ready, it's too hard"—could be called small doubts. After some practice we can learn to work skillfully with them. There also arises another level of doubt, which is very useful to us. It is called the Great Doubt, the deep desire to know our true nature or the meaning of love or freedom. The Great Doubt asks, "Who am I?" or "What is freedom?" or searches for the end of suffering. This doubt is a source of energy and inspiration in practice and is akin to the factor of enlightenment called investigation. A spirit of true investigation and inquiry is essential to enliven and deepen our spiritual practice, to keep it from being imitative. Working with the spirit, we can even find that buried within each difficulty is hidden treasure. The difficulties of doubt can lead to the discovery of our Great Doubt. The hurt of anger can lead us to a deeper sense of strength and love, and underlying restlessness is a source of spaciousness and peace.

The path of awakening is our great and wondrous legacy as human beings. It will often be difficult and at times seem almost impossible. Thomas Merton writes, "True love and prayer are learned in the hour when love becomes impossible and the heart has turned to stone." When we remember this, the difficulties we encounter in practice become themselves part of the fullness of meditation, a place to learn and to open the heart. They are the juice, part of what makes us alive. Working with these hindrances will lead us to great insight and great understanding.

So the purpose of practice is not to create a special state of mind. That is always temporary. It is to work directly with the most primary elements of our experience, all the aspects of our body, our mind, to see the way we get trapped by our fears and desires and anger and to learn directly our capacity for freedom. If we work with them, the hindrances will enrich our lives. They have been called manure for enlightenment, and some teachers speak of them as "mind weeds," which we pull up and bury near the plant to give it nourishment. Our practice is to use all that arises within us for the growth of understanding, compassion, and freedom.

J.K.

EXERCISE

Making the Hindrances Part of the Path

Choose one of the most frequent and difficult mind states that arise in your practice, such as irritation, fear, boredom, lust, doubt, or restlessness. For one week in your daily sitting be particularly aware each time this state arises. Watch carefully for it. Notice how it begins and what precedes it. Notice if there is a particular thought or image that triggers this state. Notice how long it lasts and when it ends. Notice what state usually follows it. Observe whether it ever arises very slightly or softly. Can you see it as just a whisper in the mind? See how loud and strong it gets. Notice what patterns of energy or tension reflect this state in the body. Become aware of any physical or mental resistance to experiencing this state. Soften and receive even the resistance. Finally sit and be aware of the breath, watching and waiting for this state, allowing it to come, and observing it like an old friend.

4

SUFFERING

The Gateway to Compassion

THE NATURE OF COMPASSION is a strong feeling in the heart to help others be free of their suffering. It is a wholesome movement of the mind and body that seeks to alleviate the pain and suffering of beings. Compassion is the spontaneous response of an open heart.

We don't have to look far to see how pervasive suffering is in the world. There is the suffering that people are experiencing right now due to poverty and injustice. The presence of starvation, disease, and oppression stringently defines many people's lives.

As we pay attention to the world around us, we see how evident suffering is in so many arenas of life—in politics, economics, social structures, religious conflict, interpersonal relationships, in our own minds and bodies. It is vital that we remain connected and sensitive to this fact.

Even when we live on an island of relative peace and abundance, as many of us do, if we look closely at our own lives we can see the suffering that is always present, although sometimes disguised. There is the inevitable pain of the body: disease, decay, and death are an inherent part of the process of life. It is not a question of whether this happens to one person and not to another. If we have a body, it is going to get sick and older and die.

And when we pay careful attention to the mind, we also experience many different kinds of unease. Although we may find comfort and security in the habits and routines of our lives, beneath the comfortable surface there are often vague and disquieting feelings that there is something fundamentally incomplete or unclear or not quite right about our lives. There may be an uncertainty or a feeling of hollowness that drives us to fill our time with an activity. We might feel fragmented or dissatisfied or imprisoned. At times there are overwhelming feelings of anxiety, fear, depression, anger, jealousy, lust, and so forth. What is the source of these feelings? If we are to come to a true sense of wholeness, where compassion is the natural expression of our understanding, then we must be willing to honestly investigate these aspects of ourselves.

Seeing the suffering in the world around us and in our own bodies and minds, we begin to understand suffering not only as an individual problem, but as a universal experience. It is one of the aspects of being alive. The question that then comes to mind is: If compassion arises from the awareness of suffering, why isn't the world a more compassionate place? The problem is that often our hearts are not open to feel the pain. We move away from it, close off, and become defended. By closing ourselves off from suffering, however, we also close ourselves to our own wellspring of compassion. We don't need to be particularly saintly in order to be compassionate. Compassion is the natural response of an open heart, but that wellspring of compassion remains capped as long as we turn away from or deny or resist the truth of what is there. When we deny our experience of suffering, we move away from what is genuine to what is fabricated, deceptive, and confusing.

Pain

How does this movement away from suffering happen in our lives? What is it that we stay closed to? If we become aware of how we stay closed, we are already beginning the process of opening. One of the things we close ourselves to is sensations of physical pain. We don't like to feel them, and so the mind devises various strategies of avoidance. These strategies are often clearly revealed in meditation practice. One way we avoid the reality of painful feelings is by ignoring them and pretending they don't exist. This works for a while, but eventually the pain may become too great to ignore. The mind's next tactic might be to give the pain an occasional sidelong glance; that is, we're mindful of the breath, and just out of the corner of our mental eye we glance at the pain. This still is not opening to it with awareness and compassion, allowing ourselves to feel it fully. A yet more subtle form of resistance is the "project mentality," in which we are willing to be with the pain, but we are with it in order for it to go away. With this "in order to" attitude, or sense of anticipation, we are still not relating directly; we're pushing at the pain in the guise of awareness rather than truly accepting it.

When there is resistance in the mind, compassion cannot arise, because we have in some way closed ourselves off from what is present. In the case of physical pain, our conditioned responses and habits of mind can easily be seen. They range from these subtleties of manipulation to the extreme of panic and denial. If we cannot relate directly and compassionately with our own pain during meditation, how can we do so with other, more intense sufferings that we find in ourselves, in others, and in the world? An important aspect of our dharma practice consists in clearly comprehending suffering and our conditioned reactions to it, and practicing opening to what is unpleasant instead of turning away from it. In this sense the practice of awareness is the practice of compassion; we allow ourselves to feel what is there with openness, connecting directly to each moment's experience.

Unpleasant Emotions

Just as with physical pain, there is also a broad range of difficult or unpleasant emotional states and feelings that we don't accept and from which we remain cut off. This often causes fundamental splits in our minds and can create deep psychological conflicts in our lives. Feelings of vulnerability, loneliness, unworthiness, fear—these come to us at times as part of life experience. But how often can we actually be accepting of these feelings? Our habit is to react to unpleasant emotional states in the same way we react to unpleasant physical sensations. When a feeling of loneliness arises, we don't accept it. We feel aversion, we condemn it, and we try to push it away. How much of what we do in our lives is simply an effort to avoid loneliness or boredom? The unwillingness to be with and experience these feelings keeps us always reaching or grasping for something else. How much simpler it would be to just allow these feelings, letting them arise and pass away without struggle or resistance.

One of the most difficult emotional states we experience is the feeling of insecurity, of being vulnerable. What would it be like to be totally open? We think that if others saw us as we know ourselves to be, we wouldn't be loved or respected, that people would judge us harshly, that we'd lose all our friends. The fear of being vulnerable causes us to construct a self-image that we present to the world, one that we hope it will accept and love. We put that image out in front, while the dark, murky, unacceptable part of ourselves lurks behind.

When we investigate the fear of being judged, of not being accepted, we see that it does not have to do primarily with other people; instead, it has to do with our own unwillingness to experience certain of our feelings and emotions. It is we who are judging ourselves, not accepting ourselves, not loving ourselves.

If we can allow ourselves to feel vulnerable and insecure when that is what is arising, if we can be totally ourselves without any pretense, we will find a great inner strength. It is in just that moment when we acknowledge our shadow side, the side that we have kept hidden and under wraps, that our armor loosens. It becomes possible to breathe a little more freely. We begin to open the door of compassion, for ourselves and for the human condition.

Just as the mind has devised different

ways of closing to physical pain, there are also different ways we are conditioned to avoid emotional suffering: denial, frantic activity, self-images. One of the most powerful conditioning factors in the mind that keeps us closed to what is true is the feeling of fear. Although we have been deeply conditioned by fear, for the most part we have avoided directly exploring its nature, and because we are not aware of its workings, it is often an unconscious driving force in our lives. The Taoist sage Chuang Tzu said, "Little fears cause anxiety, and big fears cause panic." When fear arises, whether it's fear of pain, fear of certain emotions, or fear of death, our practice is then opening to the feeling of fear itself. What does it feel like? What are the sensations in the body? Where are they located? Are there images or pictures in the mind? We look closely to see what is the constellation of experience we call fear, to understand its true nature. We begin to see that fear is also a passing conditioned experience and that as we open to it with greater allowance and compassion, there is less identification with it as being "I" or "mine." It becomes much more workable.

From this foundation of awareness and acceptance, we can make choices about how to act with some degree of discriminating wisdom. Sometimes it is wise to retreat from a situation, and sometimes we move ahead despite the fear. We become more willing to take some risks because our energy is not so bound up in resisting feeling the fear itself. We learn that it is okay to feel fear. Our practice should challenge us to come to the edge of what we're willing to be with, what we're willing to do, what we're willing to open to. If we keep avoiding the feeling of fear, then we have to build barriers and defenses, closing ourselves off from every experience where fear might arise. Not only is this impossible to do, but it results in a narrow and restricted way of living. We close our hearts and close off the possibility of compassion.

As well as resisting painful sensations and emotions, we also resist difficult people and unpleasant situations. There are certain people we just don't like or situations that make us uneasy. Usually, when we find people to be unpleasant or abrasive, we react to their behavior and personality and get caught up in the dynamic of resistance, of shutting them out. But if we can drop beneath the behavioral level and allow ourselves to open to others—which sometimes can happen by simply looking at them caringly, without reaction—we can often see the suffering underneath. We can get a sense, perhaps, of that place of pain in them that is manifesting, often unconsciously, as unpleasant or obnoxious behavior. And when we open to and feel the suffering of another, compassion will have the chance to come forth.

Fear of Death

Another aspect of our lives that we do not often bring to full awareness is the existential transiency of all experience. Every aspect, every element of our bodies and minds—sensations, thoughts, sense impressions, emotions, fantasies—every element of the world around us, is in constant change and flux, subject to birth, decay, and death. In our Western culture, we don't often look very closely at the face of death. We don't like to look at the process of decay and aging, and we rarely contemplate a dead body. One traditional Buddhist meditation is the contemplation of corpses in various states of decomposition. At first thought, this may seem morbid or extreme; yet it is one way of opening us to the reality of death, to the truth of what happens to the body, taking us beyond cosmetic pretentions. For many of us there may be a strong fear of dying. What is this fear of death about? When we don't clearly understand the nature of our mind and body, this fear and resistance to looking at decay and death may be very strong. We think that this mind-body is something solid and secure, that it is the person who we are—self, me, I. Naturally, when we have this viewpoint, the possibility of the death of "I," the death of self, can be frightening; it feels like a betrayal of our innermost beliefs about who we are and who is in control.

But as we open to the nature of the mind-body process, we see that it is literally—not metaphorically—being born and dying in every moment. We see that there is nothing solid, nothing static, nothing steady that goes from one year to the next, one month to the next, one moment to the next. The mind-body is a flux of constant creation and dissolution. Think for a moment of what your experience actually is from moment to moment: a sound, a sight, a thought, a sensation, an emotion, a smell, a taste. Moment to moment, these experiences arise and vanish, are being born and dying; the very nature of the process is constant, immediate, and continuous change. There is no possibility of holding on, although sometimes we try very hard to do so. When we experience this process of change in a very immediate and intimate way, then the fear of death begins to dissolve, because we see that there never has been anything solid or secure. We no longer consider death some kind of failure, apart from the natural order of things. We can be more at peace.

Opening The Heart

These are some examples of the kinds of suffering we may resist or close off to in our lives. For genuine compassion to arise it is necessary to reverse the conditioned tendency of avoidance and to open-heartedly experience the full range of our human condition. A beautiful expression of this possibility is found in the poetry of Ryokan, a wandering Zen monk who was born in the mid-eighteenth century. His poetry reflects a great willingness to be with what the Taoists call "the ten thousand joys and the ten thousand sorrows." And from this open-heartedness to all experience flows a deep and boundless compassion. These are some of the poems of Ryokan:

> Once again the children and I are
> fighting a battle using spring
> grasses.

Now advancing, now retreating, each
 time with more refinement.
Twilight—everyone has returned
 home;
The bright, round moon helps me to
 endure the loneliness.

The Autumn nights have lengthened
And the cold has begun to penetrate
 my mattress.
My sixtieth year is near,
Yet there is no one to take pity on
 this weak old body.
The rain has finally stopped; now just
 a thin stream trickles from the roof.
All night the incessant cry of insects:
Wide awake, unable to sleep,
Leaning on my pillow, I watch the
 pure bright rays of sunrise.

O, that my priest's robe were wide
 enough to gather up all the
 suffering people
In this floating world.

Why don't we, like Ryokan, open to all the joys and sorrows, to what is true in our lives? We stay closed to the full range of our experience because of a basic ignorance—an ignoring of the true nature of phenomena. We believe that happiness lies in the experience of pleasurable feelings, ignoring their fleeting, unfulfilling nature. This ignorance feeds the craving in the mind for more and more pleasant feeling. And although our desire for pleasant feeling is continually being gratified, we are never fully satisfied, precisely because of the fleetingness and insubstantiality of these feelings. The conditioning that is then happening in our minds is simply the nourishing and strengthening of desire, since, remaining unsatisfied, we are continuously wanting more. It is like trying to quench your thirst by drinking ocean water. The more you drink the thirstier you become.

An inevitable component of desire for pleasant feelings is the desire to avoid painful ones. Believing that our happiness lies in experiencing more and more pleasant feelings, we close ourselves to the full range of what arises in our lives. This ignorance and craving closes us off to an open awareness of suffering, and closes us off to compassion. Instead, the quality of compassion is subverted into sorrow. In sorrow there is an aversion to the suffering rather than an openness to it. Some people might believe that this aversion to suffering is the central motivation behind taking actions to alleviate it. But as we pay careful attention and begin to distinguish compassion from sorrow, we understand that in true compassion there is no attachment and no aversion; and that it is this state of openness to suffering which is in fact the greatest motive of skillful and effective response.

Compassionate Action

Wisdom replaces ignorance in our minds when we realize that happiness does not lie in the accumulation of more and more pleasant feelings, that gratifying craving does not bring us a feeling of wholeness or completeness. It simply leads to more craving and more aversion. When we realize in our own experience that happiness comes not from reaching out but from letting go, not from seeking pleasurable experience but from opening in the moment to what is true, this transformation of understanding then frees the energy of compassion within us. Our minds are no longer bound up in pushing away pain or holding on to pleasure. Compassion becomes the natural response of an open heart.

We can see this very immediately and directly in our meditation. When we settle back and open to what's happening in each moment, without attachment or aversion, we are developing a compassionate attitude toward each experience. From this attitude that we develop in our practice, we can begin to manifest true compassionate action in the world.

There is no particular model for what form this action should take. The whole world becomes a field for compassion, beginning with ourselves and embracing all beings. Some people are moved to help alleviate the physical suffering of others, whether due to disease or poverty or injustice. Others may feel more responsive to the mental grief or anguish that people experience. And our response itself can be so varied, from a very direct intervention in a situation, to a creative work of art, to a vibration of love in the heart. Becoming a more loving person in our everyday relationships may be one of the most compassionate actions we can do—simply becoming a little kinder.

Compassion grows from proximity to suffering. It is a response to the obvious suffering that we can observe in the world around us, and it is a response to understanding the very deepest causes of our bondage. The Buddha's great compassion could bathe the festering sores of a dying monk, and to that very same monk teach the way to final freedom. Walking on the path of enlightenment becomes itself the greatest act of compassion, because it awakens in us an understanding of the deepest levels and root causes of suffering.

This understanding fosters and nourishes a compassion that is not limited to particular people or situations. We may have compassion for the victims of social or political injustice, but can we feel compassion for those who perpetrate that injustice? Our tendency might be to feel a righteous anger toward such people, forgetting that their actions are coming out of an ignorance which is not only causing pain to others, but which is sowing the karmic seeds of their own future suffering. Can our compassion recognize that ignorance and embrace them as well?

A poem by the Vietnamese Zen master and peace worker Thich Nhat Hanh expresses very beautifully the possibility of all-embracing compassion, without boundary and without discrimination. There is a seeing that all of it, all of life, is in us, and that we can relate to it all with an open heart.

Please Call Me by My True Names

Do not say that I'll depart tomorrow
because even today I still arrive.

Look deeply; I arrive in every second
to be a bud on a spring branch,

to be a tiny bird, with wings still
fragile learning to sing in my new
nest,
to be a caterpillar in the heart of a
flower,
to be a jewel hiding itself in a stone.

I still arrive, in order to laugh and to
cry,
in order to fear and to hope,
the rhythm of my heart is the birth
and death
of all that are alive.

I am the mayfly metamorphosing on
the surface of the river,
and I am the bird which, when
spring comes, arrives in time to
eat the mayfly.

I am a frog swimming happily in the
clear water of a pond,
and I am the grass-snake, who,

approaching in silence, feeds itself
on the frog.
I am the child in Uganda, all skin and
bones,
my legs as thin as bamboo sticks,
and I am the arms merchant, selling
deadly weapons to Uganda.

I am the twelve year old girl, refugee
on a small boat,
who throws herself into the ocean
after being raped by a sea pirate,
and I am the pirate, my heart not yet
capable of seeing and loving.

I am a member of the Politburo with
plenty of power in my hands,
And I am the man who has to pay his
debt of blood to my people dying
slowly in a forced labor camp.

My joy is like spring, so warm it
makes flowers bloom in all walks
of life.

My pain is like a river of tears, so full
it fills all four oceans.
Please call me by my true names,
So I can hear all my cries and laughs
at once,
So I can see that my joy and pain are
one.

Please call me by my true names
So I can wake up and so the door of
my heart can be left open,
The door of compassion.

J.G.

EXERCISE
Cultivating Compassion

There are many levels on which we can strengthen and awaken compassion in our lives. We can practice it in silence as we sit. When thoughts or images of the suffering of other beings arise, either spontaneously or by intentionally calling them to mind, bring your attention to the area of the heart, letting yourself be touched by their pain and allowing a response of loving care and concern. Repeating the phrase "May you be free of suffering" also helps to develop the feeling of compassion within us. This phrase is directed toward the person who is suffering, and can be repeated for a few minutes or for an entire sitting period. Similarly, we can develop compassion toward ourselves when we feel our own suffering arise in meditation.

Outwardly, we can strengthen our response of compassion by working with another person. When you find yourself with someone in physical or emotional pain, take some time to be with that person, quietly if possible. Observe carefully all the different reactions that may arise in your mind and heart. Let all the movements of mind arise and pass away until there remains some inner space and silence. Look directly at the other person with a simple attitude of basic warmth. Can you see the other as a fellow human being in pain? Can you allow yourself to be touched by him or her? Is there a sense of connection or separation? Is the heart open or closed? Allow yourself to see and feel the other with the wish that he or she be free of suffering. If you can, stay with this process until you feel a sense of connection and compassion.

5

INTEGRATING PRACTICE

How can we develop and deepen our practice in the midst of our everyday lives? These are important questions. They require that we develop an integrated awareness of all dimensions of our being, making our body, our actions, our feelings and our relationships, our work and our play, all part of our meditation.

This book, based on talks given at several intensive meditation retreats, has focused primarily on the deepening of the inner meditative process, the hindrances one encounters, skillful means of mastering them, and the understandings and wisdom that can arise while in meditative silence. To integrate this understanding into our lives and actions is the whole second half of practice. To do it justice would require another entire book, devoted to the principles and laws of living an integrated and dharmic life. Still, we can touch on some of the basic guidelines here.

Whether we are sitting in formal meditation or living the dharma in action, practice is never a matter of learning formulas or imitating others. Of course, it is essential that we honor the fundamental principles of virtue and of training the mind. But we must also be willing to leap into the unknown in each new moment. And that requires courage and simplicity. Don Juan says that only with courage can we withstand the path of knowledge. He describes the world as mysterious, awesome, and unfathomable, and says that we must assume responsibility for being in this marvelous world. Since we will be here for only a short while, we must learn to make every act count.

To live our spiritual path fully offers us something beyond merely getting through life on automatic pilot. We can honor and fulfill, even ennoble, our life through the skill of our attention and the power of our heart. But it requires practice and the willingness to extend our awareness over and over again to new areas of our life.

Though this process is not always easy, it is very simple. It is learning to live in the ever-changing reality of the present moment. A woman who went to Asia many years ago and came back as a master of meditation put it this way as she was washing the lunch dishes: "Isn't it strange that we prefer the quicksand of somethingness to the firm ground of emptiness?" What an extraordinary thing to say! This capacity to be open to the new in each moment without seeking a false sense of security is the true source of strength and freedom in life. It allows us to receive all things, to touch all things, to learn from whatever presents itself. Every single situation of our life can be our teacher, can instruct us and give us the opportunity for growing fuller in our love and more understanding in our wisdom. This makes meditation a lifelong process of opening, growing, investigating, and discovering. If we ask ourselves what is the lesson for us in the situation at hand (however difficult), we will always find value.

Living fully means jumping into the unknown, dying to all our past and future ideals, and being present with things just as they are. This can be frightening, but it is only by such surrender to the moments of truth that we can participate fully in the mystery of our lives. It is a challenge we face again and again in our practice, in our relationships, and throughout each day. Meeting it requires courage.

We can see the need for letting go in our formal meditation practice, and it becomes even clearer as we end our sitting periods. When we get up, what can we hold on to? At the end of a period of silent retreat, almost all students know the experience of losing the quiet states that developed so slowly in meditation. We cannot hold on to them. As we enter the business of the marketplace, concentration and tranquillity usually dissolve, and even the power of our mindfulness diminishes. The greatest of our spiritual experiences becomes only a memory. When one Western student described to an Asian teacher all of the important experiences of his years of practice, the only response he got was, "Oh, something more to let go of."

Wisdom does not arm us with new

knowledge or armor us with spiritual power. If anything, it leaves us more open and vulnerable, to be touched by and in touch with all the things around us. Coming out of a deep inner meditation into a busy world, we often sense this vulnerability. Those who return from long retreats face the unfamiliar and difficult task of integration while feeling this profound sensitivity. At times we get overwhelmed. This process too requires practice, in and out of retreat, in and out of sitting, going back and forth from stillness to action again and again, until the spirit of the stillness pervades the action and the aliveness fills the stillness. Yet vulnerability is not the end of wisdom. Wisdom leads us even deeper, to transparency and balance. While we are vulnerable in our openness, there is still a sense of "me" and "mine," of fear and hurt. These come from deep and subtle attachments. Although they will not vanish easily, in our practice we can become aware of them and begin to sense an even deeper level of transparency, a possibility of allowing all things to arise and pass with ease.

Naturally that aspect of life which is pain and suffering will not just disappear as we practice. In fact, it will actually become more evident through our awareness. This is true of the outward sufferings of the world, and it is even more true of ourselves. There will be times when our habits will become more fully revealed—as if we are seeing them clearly for the first time. Our fears, our greeds, the aspects of our personality that we reject will wait for us like comfortable old clothes to be put on at the end of a retreat. It can be quite discouraging after touching a new level of peace or purity in the heart to see the power of our old habits. But this is just the place for the application of our practice.

We are asked to relate with understanding instead of judgment, to see with love and awareness. There is freedom, there is justice to be discovered and to manifest, and we can learn to truly embody these. But it is a process that is learned and takes place as much out of retreat as in meditative silence. It is through encountering and facing our very habits and fears, our confusion and doubts, that we discover how to apply the simplicity and power of mindfulness and letting go in all of life.

A story about Achaan Chaa is relevant here. Soon after arriving at the monastery, a new monk became frustrated by the difficulties of practice, by the seemingly arbitrary rules of conduct, and of course by his own doubts. He went to Achaan Chaa and complained about the practice and behavior of the other monks, and even about the teacher himself. He said, "You don't seem so enlightened to me. One day you say one thing, the next day you say something entirely different. If you're enlightened, why do you contradict yourself all the time?"

After a good laugh, Achaan Chaa explained that his teaching was to help people come to a balance of heart and mind. "It is as though I see people walking down a foggy road that I know very well," he said. "When I see someone about to fall into the ditch on the right-hand side I call out, 'Go left, go left.' And if I see someone about to fall off to the left, I yell, 'Go right, go right.' That is all I do."

Dharma practice is a matter of balance. If you become attached or confused and fall off to the side, let go of whatever you are clinging to and come back to center. Keep it very simple. With awareness every situation is an opportunity to strengthen this balance of mind. This balance is the central teaching of the Buddha. In fact, it was the very first phrase he used to describe the teachings—the Middle Way.

It is important to realize that to identify oneself as a meditator or a spiritual person or even a Buddhist can be another way we get caught or lose our true balance. This is like carrying a raft on your head instead of using it for a vehicle to the other shore. The purpose of meditation is not to create a new spiritual identity, nor to become the most meditative person on the block, who tells other people how they should live. To practice is to let go.

One woman who returned home after meditating at the Naropa Institute Buddhist University encountered much hostility in her parents. They were fundamentalist Christians and believed she was possessed or had joined a cult. After much struggle with them and in herself, she discovered a way to work with the situation, which she shared with the teacher. She wrote, "My parents hate me when I'm a Buddhist, but they love me when I'm a buddha!" There is no need to become a Buddhist—only to discover and embody the compassion, understanding, and freedom of spirit that is the Buddha within us.

In reading the ancient texts, we find that the essential teachings of the Buddha are not complicated at all. One sutra tells of a man who, having heard about the Buddha's great wisdom, set out to seek his teaching. After a long journey, the man finally came upon the Buddha while he was collecting alms. The man asked for teaching, but the Buddha requested that he wait until the end of his alms rounds. After having come so great a distance, the man was in no mood to wait. The man persisted, and in response to his third request, the Buddha explained the essence of his teachings succinctly and simply as they stood in the street: "In the seeing, there is only the seen. In the hearing, there is only the heard. In the sensing, there is only the sensed. In the thinking, there is only the thought." That's Buddhism in a nutshell. It is both the beginning and the end of practice.

The truth is simple, but we often complicate things. All experience is just the play of elements of sight, sound, smell, taste, touch, and thought. In them is no self, no other, no separation, and no grasping. Seeing this brings freedom. Practicing with this spirit of simplicity cuts through the web of mental entanglements, allowing us to see things clearly and directly.

There are four kinds of simplicity that are of great help in this process of coming to understand and live the truths of the dharma. The first is simplicity of body. In the sitting practice this means working with awareness of the breath, sensations, posture, and movement with a gentle and allowing attitude. We need to let ourselves settle into a posture in which we can sit comfortably yet remain alert, erect, and still. In feeling any points of tension in the body, allow them to soften and relax. Let the shoulders drop, let the breath settle, and release any tightness in the neck, back, and facial muscles. While we sit, we allow ourselves to feel whatever is happening in the body, settling into it with awareness and balance of mind. We can practice bringing this same awareness to the whole range of our activities as we move throughout the day, staying grounded in our bodies. Awareness of the body is like a mirror that can instantly show us our tension and attachments and indicate where to relax and let go. A simple and basic honoring of our bodily needs for regular exercise and a healthy diet also contributes greatly to our well-being and to a wakeful, balanced spiritual life. Living attentively and simply in the body requires a balance. On one side we must learn to respect the body and be kind to ourselves, attentive to our needs. Yet we must do so without dissipating energy by indulging every whim that arises. A traditional image used to illustrate this balance is that of a well-tuned lute, its strings neither too loose nor too tight. Experiment with diet, with regular exercise, with bodily awareness to see what works best for you. And when you get off center, which may be quite often at first, don't judge yourself. Be aware that you are off center and return to balance.

A second area of simplicity in practice is simplicity of action, developed by a simple attention to the area of the heart. In form, it is the virtue of following the precepts. Even more directly, it is an attention to the heart, to extending our caring through basic kindness and nonharming toward the world around us. There is a process of learning to be aware when our heart is open or closed and nourish that which allows for the opening. Like a flower, the heart has many cycles, and we will discover how it closes at night or in times of cold. We need to love and respect these times too. Yet even with the most difficult of these cycles, the simplicity of virtue arises when we keep our actions connected with our heart.

A third simplicity is that of our lifestyle, what has been called a life of voluntary simplicity. This too can be cultivated, especially as we recognize that busyness, entanglements, and complexities are unnecessary for our happiness. In fact, for most of us, the fewer complexities and attachments we have, the more happily and contentedly we can live. This simplicity is the basis for those who find joy in the way of the monk and nun. Naturally for householders it does not mean dropping our jobs or family responsibilities. But we can look at our life, at how complexly or fancily we live, and to see if some simplification would not lead to a quieter mind and a more contented heart. After all, we are just "accountants in the firm" anyway. We don't really keep or possess things: even our bodies are not ours. We are given them to use, and the more skillfully and simply we relate to them, the more contented our life becomes.

The fourth area of simplicity is inward, a simple relation to the mind. Our opinions rise and fall like the seasons. Our moods and thoughts come and go like the tide. What meditation practice can teach us is a simpler and wiser relationship to all changing states. The laws of the dharma are quite simple ones. All things are in change. How we act and think creates new habits and conditions for how we will act and think in the future. How we act now creates what reactions the world will return to us. This is the law of Karma. What we sow, we will reap. The amount of our attachments will equal the amount of our sufferings. The principles are direct and simple. Achaan Chaa used to ask his disciples, "Are you suffering much today?" If they said no, he would smile and move on. If they said yes, he would respond, "Oh, you must be attached," and then smile and move on. It is like the warning light on our dashboard. When the suffering light comes on, it is wired directly to how much we are attached. There is where we can learn to let go.

To relate simply is to see what is directly in front of us. As one master told his students when he died, "Friends in the dharma, do not put any false heads above your own." (Do not get caught in spiritual grasping or ideals.) "Then moment after moment watch your step closely." That is all.

We can look at practice as a process of developing sensitivity. The essence of moral virtue is sensitivity to our environment: honoring and living harmoniously with our beings and the world we share. Concentration is also sensitivity: focusing and tuning the mind to listen to what Kabir calls "the ringing of the anklets on the feet of an insect when it walks." Wisdom is sensitivity to the movements and ever-changing elements of our experience. Compassion and appreciation grow from the silence and sensitivity of our minds and hearts.

All things teach us if we are sensitive. In each moment the laws governing the dynamic play of elements of mind and matter are being revealed. Each moment is teaching about impermanence and emptiness. If we listen carefully, we can learn from the most subtle whispers of thought and sensation as well as the most overwhelming feelings and emotions. Every movement of the mind is a teaching.

This is true whether we are engaged in formal, intensive meditation practice or facing the challenges of our daily lives. Insight can develop in any circumstance; all situations can be used to deepen our understanding and the sense of magic and beauty in our experience.

Of course the same hindrances and barriers we encounter in sitting meditation will arise as we open to the world around us. There will be doubt and aversion, desire, laziness, and restlessness in relationships, in work, in all of the intimate ventures of our life. Our ideals and fears will all appear to be blocking our great openness. Yet, each of these obstacles is also our practice and the very key to our freedom.

Fear is a good example. At first fear appears as a inhibition to appreciating the moment. We're afraid to feel, to be with things fully. We're often frightened by difficult emotions, thoughts, and situations. When they arise we try to look away or stand back from them. When we do so, our relationship to the world of experience feels fragmented and shallow. Yet fear is equally a sign of growth. Fear tells us we are moving into new territory. Fear is the membrane between what we know and something new. It tells us we are about to open to something bigger than the world we usually experience. The difficulties and mysteries of life are inseparable. The whole process of discovery of the truth requires an opening to the whole of life, and our fear is a sign of opportunity as much as a problem. When we begin practice, we are afraid of making mistakes. Later we can discover that all greatness comes first from error. This is actually how we learn. As one meditation master put it, "Life is one continuous mistake."

Like fear, attachment to our ideas and opinions can also be a barrier to opening. One Zen tradition tells us to cultivate a "don't-know" mind, and another counsels the wisdom of "beginner's mind." All this is a cure for the times when we become stuck in our knowledge, our views, our way. At the opening of a beautiful and elegantly crafted Korean-American Zen temple, some devoted Korean ladies brought food and flowers as an offering to the Buddha. The flowers, however, were plastic and after the group left the American students snatched them off the altar and stashed them away. The Zen master told them to put the flowers back on the altar right away. He said that the problem was not the plastic in the flowers but the plastic in the students' minds. Because they were stuck in their ideas about beauty, they missed seeing the sincere love and devotion that the offering expressed.

We can get so caught up in our projects and plans to get the most out of situations that our vision becomes narrow. We don't appreciate the bigger picture that we are a part of because all our attention is focused upon our own little dramas. There is a story about a coyote who figured out how to dig up traps and turn them over. He evidently enjoyed this procedure because he did it often. One day a trapper buried a trap upside down, and when the coyote turned it over, he caught himself. He was smart enough to dig up traps, but not smart enough to leave them alone. Like him, we can become the victim of our own cleverness.

It is not necessary that our perception of life be so hindered by habits of judgment and evaluation and of liking and disliking. We can learn an appreciation and letting go of those habitual judgments and preferences that render our perception stale and lifeless. We can learn to see with freshness and sensitivity.

At times being sensitive can mean observing the details of experience, at other times it can mean opening the mind with an awareness that includes everything within it. Once when some geese flew by during a meditation retreat of Sasaki-roshi, he remarked: "Most people want to capture these birds and cage them. They're so beautiful, they want them. You must develop a mind which sees you and the birds as the same—not just sees it but feels it. You see and hear the birds, you are one with them. There is no need to capture or hold on to anything because you are everything."

When we let go of whatever we are clinging to, we can appreciate each thing as it is. There is no scarcity of things to appreciate but only a scarcity of moments when we are capable of truly seeing because of how often we are unaware, unmindful. Beauty arises from presence of mind and simplicity. Though our minds may be complicated, beauty is not. We don't have to strive to make beauty in our lives, or look far to find it. When the mind is still, we can see a magnificence in even the most ordinary things—the vividness of a sunset, the warmth of a smile, the simplicity of serving a cup of tea. We can see new life and growth. Each thing is different from all others, each moment is unique. And we can see decay and passing. This is the natural course of things and has its own exquisite kind of clarity.

Our perception of the richness of our experience directly reflects the depth and subtlety of our awareness. If our minds are busy and self-concerned, our sensitivity will be shallow. Many Asian arts are based on this understanding. For example, in a traditional Chinese landscape painting, the artist prepares himself through months of meditation. When the artist's mind is collected, open, and one with the object, he or she lifts the brush and the landscape paints itself.

To bring this spirit of aliveness and wakefulness into our daily life is a wonderful ideal, but it must be directly supported by the ways in which we live. There are some important methods for cultivating a strong foundation of awareness in our daily lives.

The first is to sit every day. It is one of the most important things we can do in our life. It not only provides the foundation for the deepening of our own practice, but also makes a statement with our whole being. It is a time to be silent, to listen to our heart, and to reconnect with our deeper values. The world, after all, doesn't need more things added to it. It already has enough food and enough oil and energy. What is most needed is less: less greed, less fear, less hatred, less prejudice. To sit every day is to express one's conviction in the power of silence, to open our hearts to understanding, acceptance, and genuine caring. With a strong, consistent daily sitting practice we find it easier to remain centered throughout the day's activities. Without any self-conscious effort, whatever centeredness and peacefulness grows in us will transmit itself to all those with whom we interact. Our practice is really a gift of our spirit that is naturally shared with others.

Try to sit twice a day. It is helpful to find a regular time in the morning and evening. Sitting in the morning lays a foundation of balance and awareness for the whole day. Sitting in the evening is an opportunity to let go of whatever has been accumulated during the course of the day and to let the mind and body become settled, quiet, and refreshed. If circumstances permit, sit two hours a day. If the demands of your time make this too difficult, then sit two half-hours or one hour. Find a regimen that works in the context of your life and stick to it.

For our daily practice to become consistent and for its strengths to become available to us, we cannot be idealistic about how sittings will be. Sometimes in the mornings we may be sleepy or busy anticipating the day ahead. Often in the evenings our body will be jangling and vibrating with the business of the day, and our thoughts will seem unending. If we expect peaceful and concentrated daily sittings, we won't stick with the practice for long in the face of such discouragement. Daily sitting is not like the focused practice of intensive retreat. It is a time for the stilling of the body and a balancing of the mind. Often the times we feel most unconcentrated and scattered are the times we need the most to meditate. If the body buzzes and the mind is full of thoughts, sit anyway, just make space for it to settle and discharge and try not to judge. If it gets calmer, then go back to the breath and body sensations. If we spend a whole hour unable to concentrate, fine. Just sit and take what comes. Then we will find true relation to our body, hearts, and minds.

At times we find it easy to sit every day. At other times we find that we begin to squeeze sitting into the other business of life, and eventually squeeze it out. Make the resolve not to let a day go by without sitting. If it is time to go to bed and we haven't yet sat that day, we can sit at the foot of the bed or on the floor next to it for at least a few minutes. Sometimes three minutes is enough to get back in touch with that place of balance, to come back to being centered. It can be an important reminder.

It can be helpful to create a special place in our home for sitting. This can be a room or even just a corner of your bedroom. Place there your cushion or chair or bench or whatever you sit on. If you wish, have a candle, maybe some incense, a Buddha image—whatever seems most appropriate. Perhaps you will want to keep a few of your favorite dharma books there and read them regularly to remind you of the meaning and power of practice.

Work with the walking practice, both as a formal meditation and as a way of making all actions throughout the day into meditation. Doing even a short period of walking meditation before sitting is a good way to collect yourself and get settled. And throughout the day, make the time spent walking from one place to another a time of meditation, of being balanced and present. So much of the time we are lost in our thoughts, completely unaware of our experience in the present moment. We could well be rid of ninety percent of our thoughts and still have plenty left for the useful purposes of thought. Let go of the rest. When you walk, just walk. Just be with your experience. When you get to where you are going, there will be plenty of time to plan and organize and do what you have to do.

Work with eating as a regular part of the meditation. Be aware of the diet you eat and of the way you usually take your food. Try on occasion to eat in silence, slowly and mindfully. Just to eat one apple with care and attention can be a powerful reminder of our life and practice, a way of coming back to center.

The spirit of this attention is to be present and learn from what we do, from all of the actions of body and mind. To do this is not a process of judging right and wrong. Clear seeing is aided by a sense of humor. Once the Korean Zen master Soen-sa-nim was eating breakfast and reading the morning paper at his center in Providence, Rhode Island. This upset a student who had many times heard him instruct in Zen, "When you walk, just walk" and "When you eat, just eat." How could the master say that and then go ahead and eat and read? So the student asked him about it. Soen-sa-nim looked up, smiled, and replied, "When you eat and read, just eat and read!" Our practice is to be where we actually are with love and attention.

In sustaining a life of mindfulness, it is extremely helpful to connect with other people who share the same values and orientation. Once the disciple Ananda spoke to the Buddha, saying, "It seems to me that half of the holy life is association with good and noble friends."

The Buddha replied, "Not so, Ananda. The whole of the holy life is association with good and noble friends, with noble practices, and with noble ways of living."

The support and encouragement we give one another in practice is extremely important and powerful. It's difficult to practice alone, particularly in a culture such as ours, which continually bombards us with messages saying, "Live for the future." "Do this and get that and become this and have that, and you will be happy." One of the blessings of joining a traditional community of monks and nuns is the sense of support such a sangha can give. As lay people we can find that support invaluable as well. Connecting with other people involved in spiritual practice renews our inspiration and energy. It can help keep practice alive for us in times when our motivation has waned. It can provide a way for us to support and inspire others, which itself is very strengthening to our practice.

Sit with others. If there is no sitting group meeting together regularly in your area, then start one and list it in the vipassana newspapers. If there aren't other people doing insight meditation, then sit with other Buddhist groups in your area, or sit at the local silent Quaker meetings. Joining together with anyone who understands the value of taking time to turn inward, to quiet the mind and develop awareness, is very, very helpful.

In the same way, taking periods of silence and retreat regularly throughout the year is important for the renewal and deepening of practice. Regular meditation retreats are an obvious support. So too are personal retreats alone at home or at a retreat center. Similarly days of retreat and rest in nature, hiking in the mountains or along the ocean, times of silence and listening are all nurturing to practice. It is not by accident that many of the world's greatest monasteries and spiritual centers are in forests and remote places of beauty. Silent time can renew our spirits and reconnect us with the simplicity of practice.

Just as we will discover opening and closing cycles of the heart, and up and down cycles in our meditation, there are also greater cycles of silence and service over the years of our practice. Sometimes all that we need is a quiet space in which to meditate and listen. Other cycles pull us to family life, world service, community relations—a mindful life in the world. When we work with developing a silent inner meditation, only some of what we cultivate in one area carries over to the other. Just as we must actively choose to develop consciousness in a very focused way in sitting or a panoramic way in walking, we must also choose to develop mindfulness in driving or in our relationships. In this way, we can build upon the strengths of our initial meditation practice developed in silent retreats. We can bring the power of mindfulness into all the areas of our life.

It also helps to periodically survey our lives and see what areas need more attention and consciousness. These include our work, our whole physical bodies, our diet and exercise, our intimate relationships, or our service and capacity for generosity. Wherever we are stuck or fearful or attached can become another place for our practice and growth. But we have to be willing to earnestly develop and apply the power of mindfulness and the learnings from sitting, and to purposefully bring them into all the other dimensions of our life. Naturally, some effects from the insights in our sittings and the general strengthening of equanimity and balance will carry over to all our activities. Still, even very advanced yogis, especially here in the West, have seen the need for a periodic review of their lives and the development of careful attention to areas that have been disconnected from the practice of mindfulness and the heart.

To do this also helps heal the false split between spiritual life and worldly life. Every single activity can teach us the universal laws of the dharma. We can learn as much about attachment and patience in our family as we can by observing our breath or body sensations. The universal freedom and compassion discovered by the Buddha is not far away, to be found in some distant monastery or after years of practice. It is here and now in every moment, in any activity. Where mindfulness leads us is just here, the eternal and ever-changing present.

Another aspect of practice that can also help us to open more fully in our lives is the development of generosity. Think about what areas in your family, community, or global life you would like to support more fully. Begin to practice more giving there. While at some point generosity becomes the natural expression of a connected and loving heart, in our practice it, too, can be cultivated. We can actively look for opportunities to give of our time, energy, money and goods, love and our service to others. Through practice and attention we will begin to notice occasions when we hold back or fear to relate and give—and consciously begin to cultivate a more generous response. Slowly, the whole spirit and joy of giving, from tentative to brotherly to royal giving, will grow in us, and this opening will affect all the other realms of our practice as well.

Another strong support for our daily

practice is to resolutely undertake the five basic training precepts, to cultivate a life of conscious conduct. Following these precepts is a powerful way to bring mindfulness into our life. It can help to take them formally by reciting them with a teacher or reciting them out loud from a book.

Traditionally, one takes the precepts by saying, "I undertake the training precept of refraining from killing," and so on for each one. We resolve to follow and use them as guidelines to train ourselves. Then they can be taken again when we are aware of having broken one. To review them in detail, go back to the first chapter of this book. Each precept is a direct way to avoid harming ourselves and other beings. Each precept also reminds us of an area of life in which we can develop sensitivity and compassion. The strength of the precepts is very great. If even one-half of the first precept were kept worldwide—the precept to refrain from killing or from lying, for instance—it could transform our planet.

Work carefully with each of the five precepts: not killing, not stealing, refraining from sexual misconduct, not speaking falsely, not using intoxicants heedlessly. Learning to work with the precepts is the groundwork for genuine spiritual practice. If we are causing harm to others, if we are being dishonest or irresponsible, we become stuck, and it is impossible to go any further in our practice. More skillfully, we can use the precepts to train ourselves, to awaken ourselves and make our relationships more open and harmonious. When we are about to break them, the precepts are like warning lights and alarms signaling us to take a careful look at the mind state behind the action in which we are involved. If we look closely, we can usually discover where we became caught or confused and how we can let go and be free. Use the precepts. They are incomparable tools for changing ourselves and the world around us.

People often wonder about how best to share their inspiration and practice with others. Of course, it is wonderful to speak with others and about the dharma, but we need to be sensitive to the circumstances and careful to speak appropriately. There is no need to proselytize or preach, or even to mention Buddhism at all. Rather, be open to each situation. If you speak of practice at all, let it be to those who truly wish to know. Better to be a buddha than a Buddhist, and let the teachings come more from the heart and deeds than the mouth. Remember, we communicate not only with words, but with every aspect of our being. People learn more from what we are than from what we say.

Some students once asked a renowned

Tibetan Buddhist master how they could train their children to live a spiritual life. This Lama reminded them that their children have their own karma, and parents cannot force them to be a certain way. He told the parents that if they took care of their own practice, the children would learn from the kindness and clarity manifested in their example. We can say, "You should love everyone," but if we then treat the people who serve us at the gas station or supermarket as though they were part of the machinery, that unspoken message is clearly communicated. Through practice our intentions, or inspirations, our words, and our deeds can all come together. We can cultivate loving-kindness and mindfulness until they become the way we live our life. Then, when the baby cries or the knees hurt in sitting or we are stuck in traffic or someone dies, it will all become part of the dharma for us.

When the wonderful old Tibetan master Kalu Rinpoche came to the United States, he visited the Boston Aquarium. As he walked through, he would stop at each new tank of colorful fishes to observe and admire them. Then, as he left each tank, he would touch the glass softly and say the mantra "Om Mani Padme Hum." When asked why he did that, he replied, "I touch the glass to get the attention of the beings inside, and then I bless each one, that they too might be liberated." What a wonderful way to greet each being who comes into our life. To silently touch them with the heart of kindness and wish that they too might be liberated.

Our growth as individuals is a long journey, and integrating our retreat experiences into our daily lives is one of the most compelling, sensitive, and important aspects of this journey.

We can get support from retreats and

meditation practices. We can get guidance through a relationship with a teacher. Yet in the end we must discover our own path, moment after moment. We must become our own guides and our own teachers. Through our honest inquiry and wholehearted attention, the dharma will be found right here within us.

Before one Western Buddhist monk returned to America, he spoke to an old English monk who had many times gone back and forth between Europe and his monastery in Asia. The first monk had been wondering how to integrate practice in a Western context, and so he asked for some advice. The old man said, "I have just one thing to tell you. If, as you are approaching the bus stop, you see that the bus is about to leave without you, don't panic. There will be another bus."

There can be no hurry to be in the moment. There is no rush to reassume our true nature. It takes moment-to-moment patience to integrate our practice and thus transform our lives. It takes moment-to-moment patience to cultivate and nourish the heart and the mind, to nurture the blossoming of our own true nature.

Awareness, sensitivity, courage, wisdom—they are not qualities that can be forced on anyone, nor are they remote ideals to be attained someday. They can only be awakened, and once awakened within us, they spring forth spontaneously in our words and deeds, awakening the same in all whom they touch. Their communicative and transforming power is irresistible because they are the deepest truth of our being.

J.K.

EXERCISE

Strengthening Mindfulness

1. *Daily sitting log.* Here is a way to strengthen daily practice and to see its cycles more clearly. For one month or two, keep a small notebook at the place where you sit. Each day note down how long you sit. Then note down in one sentence the general qualities of the sitting such as "sleepy" or "restless and disturbed" or "calm and light" or "filled with many plans" or "easily centered on the breath," or whatever you notice. Then in another sentence or two note the general qualities of your day such as "happy" or "relaxed and spacious" or "overworked and tense" or "frustrated and anxious." At the end of a month or two, review your notes and be aware of the cycles in your daily sitting practice and how they may reflect and be

connected to your daily life. Particularly become aware of areas where you may be stuck and those which call for greater mindfulness and acceptance.

2. *Reminders to pay attention: Developing the habit of wakefulness.* This exercise lasts one month. At the beginning of each week choose a simple regular activity of your life that you usually do unconsciously, on automatic pilot. Resolve to make that particular activity a reminder, a place to wake up your mindfulness. For example, you might choose making tea, shaving, bathing, or perhaps the simple act of getting into the car. Resolve to pause for a couple of seconds before each time you begin the activity. Then do it with a gentle and full attention, as if it were the heart of a meditation retreat for you. As you go through the week, try to bring a careful mindfulness to that act each time it arises in your life. Even the simplest acts can be a powerful

reminder and bring a sense of presence and grace. If you choose the opening of doors throughout the day, you can open each door as if the Buddha himself were to pass through with you. If you choose the act of making tea or coffee, you can do it as if it were a gracious Japanese tea ceremony. At the end of the week add another activity, until by the end of the month you have included four new areas of your life into daily mindfulness. Then, if you wish, continue this exercise for a second and third month, bringing the power of attention into more and more of each day.

3. *Choosing a life of voluntary simplicity.* Do this exercise after a day or more of meditative sitting or after a day or more spent removed from civilization in nature. Sit and allow yourself to become calm and silent. Then, in a simple way, review your current life. Bring to mind each of several

major areas including your schedule, your finances and work, your relationships or family life, your home, your leisure activities, your possessions, your goals, and your spiritual life. As each area comes to mind, ask yourself the question: What would it be like to greatly simplify this area of my life? Continue to sit quietly and reflect, letting the images or answers arise for each area about which you ask. Then, after reflecting in this way, again bring to mind each area and ask a second question: If it became simpler, would I be happy?

The purpose of spiritual life is to discover freedom, to live in harmony with the world around us and our own true nature. To do so brings happiness and contentment. If any aspect of your life shows a need for simplification and if the way for this simplification shows itself to you, keep it in mind and begin the process of mindful change.

ACKNOWLEDGMENTS

We thank the following for permission to reprint material copyrighted or controlled by them: the Hanuman Foundation for "Please Call Me by My True Names" by Thich Nhat Hanh, © 1983 by Thich Nhat Hanh, reprinted from Thich Nhat Hanh, *Being Peace* (Berkeley, Calif.: Parallax Press, 1987); John Weatherhill, Inc., for the four poems by Ryokan from *One Robe, One Bowl,* trans. John Stevens, © 1977 John Weatherhill, Inc.

LIBRARY OF CONGRESS
CATALOGING-IN-PUBLICATION DATA

Goldstein, Joseph, 1944–
[Seeking the heart of wisdom. Selections]
The path of insight meditation/Joseph Goldstein and
Jack Kornfield.—1st Shambhala ed.
p. cm. —(Shambhala pocket classics)
Book consists of selected chapters from
Seeking the heart of wisdom. 1987.
ISBN 1-57062-069-5
1. Meditation—Buddhism. 2. Vipaśyanā
(Buddhism) I. Kornfield, Jack, 1945– .
II. Title. III. Series.
BQ5612.G4632 1995 95-9930
294.3′443—dc20 CIP

SHAMBHALA POCKET CLASSICS

THE ART OF PEACE:
Teachings of the Founder of Aikido
by Morihei Ueshiba
Compiled and translated by John Stevens

THE ART OF WAR by Sun Tzu
Translated by Thomas Cleary

BACKWOODS AND ALONG THE SEASHORE
by Henry David Thoreau

BECOME WHAT YOU ARE by Alan Watts

BHAGAVAD GITA
Translated by Shri Purohit Swami

THE BOOK OF FIVE RINGS
by Miyamoto Musashi
Translated by Thomas Cleary

I CHING: The Book of Change
Translated by Thomas Cleary

MEDITATION IN ACTION
by Chögyam Trungpa

THE MEDITATIONS OF MARCUS AURELIUS
Translated by George Long

SAPPHO
Translated by Mary Barnard

(Continued on next page)

SONG OF MYSELF by Walt Whitman
Edited by Stephen Mitchell

TAO TEH CHING by Lao Tzu
Translated by John C. H. Wu

TEACHINGS OF THE BUDDHA
Edited by Jack Kornfield

THOUGHTS IN SOLITUDE by Thomas Merton

THE TIBETAN BOOK OF THE DEAD
Translated by Francesca Fremantle & Chögyam Trungpa

WALDEN by Henry David Thoreau

THE WAY OF A PILGRIM
Translated by Olga Savin